As platforms like TikTok emerge, there is much to learn about the many people and ideas it gives voice to, as well as silences and suppresses. Boffone has given us a must-read collection for those working to make the pressing issues of internet culture and community legible. This work further expands the urgent need for a disciplinary field of internet studies as digital media platforms are remaking our worlds.

Safiya Umoja Noble, author of *Algorithms of Oppression*

I0123555

TikTok Cultures in the United States

TikTok Cultures in the United States examines the role of TikTok in US popular culture, paying close attention to the app's growing body of subcultures.

Featuring an array of scholars from varied disciplines and backgrounds, this book uses TikTok (sub)cultures as a point of departure from which to explore TikTok's role in US popular culture today. Engaging with the extensive and growing scholarship on TikTok from international scholars, chapters in this book create frameworks and blueprints from which to analyze TikTok within a distinctly US context, examining topics such as gender and sexuality, feminism, race and ethnicity and wellness.

Shaping TikTok as an interdisciplinary field in and of itself, this insightful and timely volume will be of great interest to students and scholars of new and digital media, social media, popular culture, communication studies, sociology of media, dance, gender studies, and performance studies.

Trevor Boffone is Lecturer in the Women's, Gender & Sexuality Studies Program at the University of Houston and a high school teacher at Bellaire High School. His work using TikTok with his students has been featured on *Good Morning America*, *ABC News*, *Inside Edition*, and *Access Hollywood*, among numerous national media platforms. He is the author of *Renegades: Digital Dance Cultures from Dubsmash to TikTok* and the co-author of *Latinx Teens: US Popular Culture on the Page, Stage, and Screen*.

Routledge Focus on Digital Media and Culture

For more information about this series, please visit: https://www.routledge.com

TikTok Cultures in the United States

Edited by
Trevor Boffone

R Routledge
Taylor & Francis Group

LONDON AND NEW YORK

First published 2022
by Routledge
4 Park Square, Milton Park, Abingdon, Oxon OX14 4RN

and by Routledge
605 Third Avenue, New York, NY 10158

Routledge is an imprint of the Taylor & Francis Group, an informa business

British Library Cataloguing-in-Publication Data
A catalogue record for this book is available from the British Library

Library of Congress Cataloging-in-Publication Data
Names: Boffone, Trevor, editor.
Title: Tiktok cultures in the United States / edited by Trevor Boffone.
Description: Abingdon, Oxon ; New York, NY : Routledge, 2022. |
Series: Routledge focus on digital media and culture | Includes
bibliographical references and index.
Identifiers: LCCN 2021062408 (print) | LCCN 2021062409 (ebook) |
ISBN 9781032246079 (hbk) | ISBN 9781032249162 (pbk) | ISBN
9781003280705 (ebk)
Subjects: LCSH: Social media—United States. | Generation Z—United
States—Social conditions. | Popular culture—United States. | Dance
and the Internet—United States.
Classification: LCC HM743.T55 T54 2022 (print) | LCC HM743.T55
(ebook) |
DDC 302.23/10973—dc23/eng/20220204
LC record available at https://lccn.loc.gov/2021062408
LC ebook record available at https://lccn.loc.gov/2021062409

ISBN: 978-1-032-24607-9 (hbk)
ISBN: 978-1-032-24916-2 (pbk)
ISBN: 978-1-003-28070-5 (ebk)

DOI: 10.4324/9781003280705

Typeset in Times New Roman
by codeMantra

Trey Christian Pokorny (2002–2021)

Contents

Contributors

Frederick Luis Aldama is the Jacob & Frances Sanger Mossiker Chair in the Humanities and Affiliate Faculty in Radio-TV-Film at the University of Texas, Austin, USA, as well as Adjunct Professor & Distinguished University Professor at The Ohio State University, USA. He is the award-winning author of over 48 books and founder and director of UT Austin's Latinx Pop Lab.

Jane Barnette is an Associate Professor in the Department of Theatre and Dance at the University of Kansas, USA, where she teaches courses in dramaturgy, theatre history and analysis, and theatrical adaptation. She is the author of *Adapturgy* and has a forthcoming book about the performance and representation of Witch characters.

Trevor Boffone is a Lecturer in the Women's, Gender & Sexuality Studies Program at the University of Houston, USA, and a high school teacher at Bellaire High School in Texas. His work using TikTok with his students has been featured on *Good Morning America*, *ABC News*, *Inside Edition*, and *Access Hollywood*, among numerous national media platforms. He is the author of *Renegades: Digital Dance Cultures from Dubsmash to TikTok* and the co-author of *Latinx Teens: US Popular Culture on the Page, Stage, and Screen*.

Cienna Davis is a doctoral student at the Annenberg School for Communication at the University of Pennsylvania in Philadelphia, USA. She completed her Masters in North American Studies at the Free University of Berlin, Germany, and double majored in Ethnic Studies and Communications at the University of California San Diego, USA.

Tom Divon is a social media and culture researcher in the Department of Communication and Journalism at the Hebrew University of

Jerusalem, Israel. Divon's research focuses on the evolution of social media platforms, social-political youth cultures on social media, and their potential for education processes. Divon examines TikTok cultures in three key areas: TikTokers engagements with Holocaust Commemoration and Education, TikTokers Performative Combat in Antisemitism, and TikTokers Memetic Participation in Nationalism-driven conflicts.

Tobias Ebbrecht-Hartmann is a Film & Media, Visual Culture, and German Studies scholar in the Department of Communication and at the European Forum of the Hebrew University of Jerusalem. He holds a PhD from the Freie University in Berlin and was a Post-Doctoral Fellow at Yad Vashem, Israel, and at the Bauhaus University in Weimar, Germany. He is a member of the Horizon 2020 Research and Innovation Action, "Visual History of the Holocaust: Rethinking Curation in the Digital Age."

Miriam Field is a grade eight student in Ontario, Canada. She enjoys social media, hanging out with her friends and family, swimming, skating, cross-country running, and listening to music. She posts videos about social justice movements, including #BLM and #97percent, and loves making fun and funny TikToks with her friends.

Elena Machado Sáez is a Professor of English at Bucknell University, USA. Most recently, she has published articles on *Hamilton*, *In the Heights*, and Lin-Manuel Miranda's Twitter feed. Machado Sáez current project, *Staging Activism in US Latinx Theater*, focuses on how Latinx playwrights depict activism and adopt archival practice as a form of activism.

Wendyliz Martinez is a current PhD student in English and African American Studies at Penn State University, USA. She is a City College of New York and Mellon Mays Undergraduate Fellow Alumni. Her research interests include Caribbean literature, Afrofuturism, and the digital humanities.

Zachary D. Palmer is an Assistant Professor in the Department of Sociology and Criminal Justice at Texas A&M University Commerce, USA. His research focuses on gender, masculinities, and pop culture.

Shauna Pomerantz is an Associate Professor of Child and Youth Studies at Brock University in Ontario, Canada. She has published books and articles on immanent girlhoods, girls and social media, feminism and post-feminism, girl power, girls' style, dress codes, computer girls, skater girls, gender and education, and girlhoods in popular culture.

Elle Rochford is a PhD Candidate in the Department of Sociology at Purdue University, USA. Her work examines inequalities, social movements, law and policy, and technology.

Claudia Skinner is a PhD student in American Studies and Culture at Washington State University's School of Languages, Cultures, and Race. She also serves as the Graduate Assistant for WSU's Undocumented Initiatives. She completed her Bachelor of Arts (Honours I) in American Studies at the University of Sydney, Australia, in 2017.

Katlin Marisol Sweeney-Romero is a PhD candidate in the Department of English at The Ohio State University who specializes in US Latinx Studies and popular culture. She is at work on her dissertation, which explores how Latina content creators use social media accounts to produce self-images and an online self.

Acknowledgments

Although I may have edited this book alone, there are a number of people who supported this collection along the way. My name may appear on the cover of this book, but it's been a collective effort.

I thank my editor Suzanne Richardson at Routledge who was incredibly enthusiastic about this project from the beginning. The entire team at Routledge was a joy to work with, making this process enriching from start to finish. Thank you to the anonymous readers whose reports were incredibly helpful and shaped much of the direction of this book.

I extend my deepest thanks to this collection's contributors, who expeditiously worked to bring this book to fruition. The process was fast and furious from the beginning. Your efforts did not go unnoticed.

I owe an enormous debt of gratitude to Carla Della Gatta, Cristina Herrera, Jessica Hinds-Bond, and Sarah Jerasa for critical feedback on several components of this book. I give a special shoutout to Crystal Abidin, Barrie Gelles, Ashleigh Green, Aria Halliday, Josh Inocéncio, Jasmine E. Johnson, Melanie Kennedy, Christian Lewis, William D. Lopez, Claire M. Massey, Margaret Owusu, and Bryan M. Vandevender for supporting this book at various stages.

Lastly, I thank my partner Kayla and our two fur babies, Pickles and Teddy. Meow.

Introduction

The Rise of TikTok in US Culture

Trevor Boffone

In June 2021, Megan Thee Stallion released a new single—"Thot Shit."
Given the recent wave of songs such as "Savage," "WAP," and "Body"
that had become hits after going viral on TikTok with dance challenges primarily choreographed by Black women, everyone looked to
TikTok to see what Black creators had in store for Megan Thee Stallion's new earworm of a song. But as TikTokers endlessly scrolled on
their For You Pages (FYPs) waiting for the next viral dance challenge,
it never materialized. While the likes of Keara Wilson had choreographed viral dance challenges—Savage, in this case—only to have
their work co-opted by ultra-famous TikTokers such as Charli D'Amelio and Addison Rae Easterling, there would be no Keara this time.
Nope. Not at all.

By summer 2021, Black TikTokers not only were aware of their
cultural capital on TikTok, but, more importantly, were collectively
working against the exploitation that had quickly become baked into
the TikTok platform itself from its debut in the United States in 2018.
Following high-profile controversies over dance credit, cultural appropriation, and Blaxploitation in the wake of the #RenegadeChallenge in
winter 2019–2020 (in which Charli D'Amelio rose to fame for a dance
challenge she didn't create) and Addison Rae's appearance on *The Tonight Show Starring Jimmy Fallon* in March 2021 (in which she taught
Fallon TikTok dances largely created by Black teens), Black TikTokers
had decided enough was enough. Rather than create the next viral
dance challenge to "Thot Shit," Black TikTokers refused to choreograph the song, effectively went on strike, and watched white TikTokers attempt to create a dance to Megan Thee Stallion's hit song. The
results were awkward videos of white teens flailing their arms in the air
and shaking their hips left-to-right even as Megan Thee Stallion clearly
offered a blueprint to the dance in the song's lyrics—"Hands on my
knees, shakin' ass, on my thot shit." Even as the sound bite did go viral

DOI: 10.4324/9781003280705-1

on TikTok, there was no noticeable dance challenge, marking a blip from the way that viral songs are matched with a viral dance challenge in the TikTok era. Although far from the only example, "Thot Shit" offered a glimpse into how conversations about anti-Blackness, white supremacy, cultural appropriation and exploitation, dance credit, and labor materialize on TikTok, something that mirrors US culture at large, not just today but historically. Accordingly, "Thot Shit" and the subsequent Black TikTok strike speaks to the varied ways that TikTok has fully penetrated mainstream culture in the United States. At the same time, this moment marked a shift in how non-TikTok users took notice of the racial politics of TikTok. The Black TikTok strike was widely discussed, from social media feeds and pop culture websites to mainstream news venues and daytime talk shows. This wasn't simply a TikTok controversy; it was a controversy about US culture itself. As TikTok goes, so, too, does the United States.

This book focuses on the United States, but TikTok's journey began far from North America. TikTok is the international answer to Chinese social media company ByteDance's enormously popular video-sharing app Douyin, which has been available in China since 2016.[1] ByteDance launched TikTok internationally in 2017. In the same year, ByteDance acquired Musical.ly, which had been popular among teenagers in the United States and United Kingdom since its launch in 2014.[2] With the Musical.ly purchase, ByteDance positioned TikTok as the next major social media app for Gen Z in the United States and beyond. Despite TikTok only becoming available to US iPhone and Android users in August 2018, it didn't take long for TikTok culture to become general US culture. Bolstered by Musical.ly's success, as soon as TikTok entered the US social media market, hordes of teenagers in the United States began migrating to the social media network. In just four years, TikTok has come to dominate the US social media market, mirroring the app's international successes.[3] TikTok has had over three billion global downloads and has around one billion active users who engage with the platform to create 3–60-second-long videos featuring a wide spectrum of aesthetic, thematic, and stylistic choices.[4] In the United States, the app is largely synonymous with Generation Z, or so-called Zoomers, given that teenagers and young 20-somethings were the first community to adopt TikTok en masse. They continue to be the platform's trendsetters, dictating TikTok's larger, mainstream culture. By 2020, the app had penetrated mainstream US culture, becoming a space for social media users of all ages. As TikTok continues to cement its place in mainstream popular culture, the need to analyze the social network's role in US culture grows. This book fills this gap.

TikTok Cultures in the United States explores how TikTok has become a cultural force in the country. The present collection considers the increasingly blurred lines between analog and digital cultures, paying specific attention to how TikTok users have innovated cultural exploration and, as a result, influenced everyday popular culture in the United States. As such, the book provides a range of frameworks from which to analyze TikTok as a cultural hotbed. Featuring an array of perspectives from distinct scholarly fields and backgrounds, *TikTok Cultures in the United States* joins the efforts of other consortiums such as the TikTok Cultures Research Network (founded by Crystal Abidin), the Global TikTok Researchers network in the United Kingdom (led by Andy Miah and Mariann Hardey), and the Race, Queerness and TikTok: Solidarity and Safety in Algorithmic Culture research cluster (led by Liz Grumbach and Sarah Florini) in further establishing TikTok itself as a field of scholarly inquiry.[5] While the aforementioned research spans the globe—the TikTok Cultures Research Network is mostly focused on Asia and the Pacific, for instance—*TikTok Cultures in the United States* is more narrowly focused. The book's geographic specificity is in recognition of the fact that the app's content, culture, aesthetics, trends, challenges, and mores vary from region to region. While the TikTok interface may be the same, a TikToker in Melbourne will have a vastly different experience than will a TikToker in Minneapolis, and TikTok in Shanghai is not the same as TikTok in San Francisco. Of course, there are overlaps, and TikTok in Asia and the South Pacific is relevant to any conversation about TikTok in North America. The authors in this collection while focusing on US culture are aware that this conversation will also be of value to those studying and learning about the app in other regions.

Given TikTok's youth, some critics may be skeptical of the need for a collection that unpacks the app's influence on US popular culture. Despite only being available since 2018, however, TikTok has shifted social media use in the country, and the way it has manifested and commanded a shift in culture warrants scholarly inquiry. This research also has implications for how future digital spaces will shape cultural literacies. Accordingly, I frame TikTok as what Raymond Williams calls a "formal innovation," or new cultural practices that push against well-established mainstream culture. In the case of Tik-Tok, it doesn't just push against culture but rather aligns and enhances it. Williams posits that many people overlook emerging cultures: "it is easy to miss their formal significance by comparison with preceding or succeeding mature examples.... It is then easy to miss one of these key elements in cultural productions: innovation as it is happening;

innovation in process."[6] TikTok is still an emerging platform, less established than Web 2.0 rivals such as Facebook, Twitter, and Instagram. TikTok is still defining itself in the United States, and US residents are still figuring out how the platform fits into the fabric of everyday life in the country. And yet, TikTok has fully penetrated US culture. Take for instance a trip to grocery chain Trader Joe's, which features an "As Seen on TikTok" section promoting foods made popular by TikTok. Or, for example, Barnes & Noble stores, with tables dedicated to #BookTok. And, of course, TikTok has perhaps had the most obvious influence on the music industry; trending songs on TikTok find commercial success and land at the top of the charts. Whether the artist is Lil Nas X, Brockhampton, Doja Cat, The Weeknd, Cardi B, Megan Thee Stallion, Bella Poarch, or The Backyardigans, TikTok holds the power to make music go viral in a way that Instagram, for example, does not. As trending "TikTok made me do it" challenges reveal,[7] TikTok has a clear and significant impact on behavior, making us eat certain foods, read new books, or listen to new music. Whether it's food, literature, or music, the examples of TikTok's role in the United States are expansive.

Although TikTok's mainstream culture (also known as "Straight TikTok") factors into this equation, the app is home to a vast array of subcultures that use the space as a critical site to shape and perform communal identities and cultures. Whether it is BookTok and its community of bookworms, DracoTok and its legion of *Harry Potter* fans, CottageCore TikTok and those romanticizing farm life, or even the app's mainstream dancing teens, TikTok builds community. *TikTok Cultures in the United States* uses these mainstream cultures and niche communities as a point of departure from which to explore TikTok's role in popular culture today.

TikTok 101

TikTok has been likened to "digital crack cocaine."[8] Jing Zeng, Crystal Abidin, and Mike S. Schäfer suggest the app's FYP is "one of the most addictive scrolling experiences on the Internet."[9] I couldn't agree more. Once we finally take the plunge and download the app, we quickly become addicted. The platform allows for mindless entertainment, pulling us in as we scroll to see what we'll get next. We need our fix, and the only way to get it is to continue to scroll TikTok, swiping up until we have lost track of time. And we are not alone. TikTok's roughly one billion active monthly users open the app about eight times per day, spending about 52 minutes per day watching and engaging with video content.[10] Although US TikTok was largely seen as a Gen Z space,[11] TikTok culture shifted at the onset of the COVID-19 pandemic in March 2020. With much of the country self-isolated at home, even on lockdown in some cases, the app's user base broadened, with the app becoming a home for users of all ages who used it to get their entertainment fix, connect socially, and, more importantly, pass the time. All of a sudden, the digital land of teenagers hitting dance challenges became one where nearly every celebrity and major brand had joined in, engaging with Gen Z culture and furthering the app's reach into US popular culture. The app has since shown a steady rise, quickly becoming one of the most downloaded apps of the 2010s and the most downloaded app in 2020 and 2021. TikTok now rivals legacy Web 2.0 apps such as Facebook, Instagram, and Twitter—and it shows no sign of slowing down.

While casual onlookers and critics will claim that "it's *just* Tik-Tok" and, consequently, irrelevant or inferior, TikTok is anything but that. Media studies scholar Andreas Schellewald recognizes how TikTok's "ephemeral video clips appearing on people's content feeds present themselves not as random and short-lived entertainment but as complex, cultural artifacts."[12] Or, as I propose in *Renegades: Digital Dance Cultures from Dubsmash to TikTok*, teens today use social media platforms like TikTok "to self-fashion identity, form supportive digital communities, and exert agency."[13] That is, TikTok is a site for "meaning-making practices" that begin on the app but quickly migrate into other digital and analog spaces in our day-to-day lives. Therefore, it isn't *just* TikTok; it *is* our culture. Our lives are increasingly intertwined between the digital and the material because we use a variety of web-based platforms to produce a digital version of everyday life. That being so, digital spaces and practices force us to reimagine our identities and sociocultural practices. In this case, TikTok informs identity formation as well as group culture. In *Digital Leisure, the Internet and Popular Culture*, Karl Spracklen suggests that the performance of culture on the digital stage charges us with reimagining our identities, the way that subcultures form, and the ways in which we engage with any number of cultural and leisurely activities.[14] TikTok is no exception.

TikTok is public pedagogy.[15] Especially considering TikTok's accessibility, it teaches us how to act, what to listen to, what to buy, how to speak, how to interact with one another, and more. We learn how to be ourselves on TikTok. We learn about music, memes, trends, and fashion. In this case, TikTok is what danah boyd calls a "cultural mindset": we use the platform as identity blueprints to mold our behaviors

to fit within the app's culture.[16] As TikTokers mimic, reenact, and reimagine the platform's trends and its influencers' activity, TikTok becomes embedded into our personalities, muddying where our online
activity ends and where our offline lives begin. And, perhaps most significantly, the public space of TikTok bolsters the status quo while also
remaining a space of resistance and disruption. TikTok is filled with
joy, escapism, pleasure, education, and community-building, even if
the platform bolsters systemic racism, classism, ableism, and the like.
As the chapters in this collection convey, TikTok can be both of these
things; there is nuance.

On TikTok, this cultural work operates in a way marked by hyper-
visibility. Scholar Kyesha Jennings recognizes that "digital spaces like
Twitter and Instagram offer the necessary tools to create meaning that
is far more visible and accessible than other spaces allow, such as a
concert setting."[17] Although Jennings is not speaking directly to Tik-
Tok here, her words ring especially true to the platform. Even more
so than Twitter and Instagram, which still give users the option to
have private profiles, TikTok is entirely public. Moreover, influenced
by Gen Z aesthetics and cultural norms, TikTok is a space where users portray an authentic, unfiltered, and incredibly public view of the
reality of their lives. Whereas Millennials grew up with anonymous
avatars and profiles on internet message boards, LiveJournal, Tumblr, and the like—often under threat by their parents to never post
identifying information about themselves online—teenage TikTokers
routinely upload videos in which they give tours of their houses, vlog
about their everyday routines, including their specific locations, and
detail where they go to school, who they are dating, where they go
to church, you name it. TikTok, then, is incredibly unfiltered and extremely public. This unfiltered, public social media activity lends itself
to the vulnerability of being silly, honest, and real—elements that are
part of the aesthetic and attraction for TikTok.

TikTok in the United States is a Gen Z space and, as such, reflects
Zoomer cultural aesthetics and more. From the beginning, TikTok
was quickly adopted as a central convening space for US teenagers
and young 20-somethings. As a result, Zoomers have used the app as
a fundamental site to construct and perform generational identity.
Writing for *Digiday*, Deanna Ting underscores how TikTok's appeal
to Gen Z lies in how "it's been designed from the very beginning; it emphasizes short-form video content, it's easy to use and it's even easier
to go viral on the app than other more established social media platforms." Moreover, TikTok "also feeds in perfectly to Gen Z's desire for
entrepreneurship and being a creator."[18] Even today, TikTok culture

is still dominated by Zoomers. Accordingly, even when Millennials, Gen X, and Boomers—or people born in the "1900s," as Gen Z would say—engage with TikTok aesthetics, trends, and cultures, they are inevitably engaging with Gen Z culture. As Gen Z goes, TikTok goes. Gen Z has given us permission to let our hair down, be weird, and go viral for it.

What Makes TikTok Tick Tock?

In *The App Generation: How Today's Youth Navigate Identity, Intimacy, and Imagination in a Digital World*, Howard Gardner and Katie Davis frame social media applications, and Web 2.0 at large, as a space for (young) people to form their identities.[19] By using apps as identity templates, youth can, in turn, create a stronger sense of self-identification. Gardner and Davis remark, "digital media open up new avenues for youth to express themselves creatively." By making use of "remix, collage, video production, and music composition,"[20] for example, young people can become creators on TikTok and other digital platforms, engage with other creators, and, ultimately, engross themselves in Tik-Tok's identity blueprint culture. So, if TikTok can be understood as an identity blueprint, then what do we make of TikTok challenges, trends, and aesthetics? How do these components of the platform factor into how TikTokers form identity, cultures, and communities? Where does this work begin on TikTok?

Ask anyone on TikTok, and they will share stories about the TikTok algorithm feeding them shockingly accurate content: videos perfectly tailored to their interests, location, and identity markers. At times, TikTok appears to know more about us than we do. Take, for instance, the trend of queer TikTokers posting videos that reveal how it took them 20 years to figure out that they were gay, whereas it took the TikTok algorithm 20 minutes. TikTok knows. Accordingly, I propose that what makes TikTok tick tock is algorithmic personalization that enables identities, communities, and cultures to take shape on the platform, a phenomenon that quickly spills into the analog world as TikTok content goes viral. As a result, TikTok becomes US culture, and US culture becomes TikTok.

Contrary to platforms like Facebook, Instagram, and Twitter, when users open TikTok, they are first met with the FYP, a stream of content that presents each user with content the app's algorithm believes is exactly right for them. TikTokers don't begin the TikTok experience by viewing content from people they follow; rather, TikToking is marked by viewing new content that is dictated by our interests and our previous interactions with the app. The more time TikTokers spend engaging with posts through repeated viewings, liking, commenting, favoriting, sharing, and downloading, the more users teach the algorithm how to better personalize their TikTok experience. Media studies scholar Andrea Ruehlicke claims TikTok "represents a new development in how we think and talk about personalization in virtual spaces."[21] Indeed, Kirsten Drotner notes,

> the enormous expansion of today's media landscape in many parts of the world and the increase in personalized media technologies have meant that young people in particular have a more diversified, individualized use of media, that closely reflects their own priorities.[22]

Even though Drotner is speaking of contemporary youth cultures in general, her words ring especially true for TikTok.

And, although TikTok permeates virtually all facets of contemporary life in the United States, oftentimes in clandestine, little-noticed ways, TikTok is also known for how it operates outside of the mainstream. That is, TikTok is home to a growing legion of cultures that materialize on the platform before spilling over into the analog world. As TikTok has grown, so too have (sub)cultures, or (sub)categories, on the app, something made possible by how the algorithm facilitates extreme personalization.[23] TikTokers are often aware not just of these Web 2.0 cultural communities but also of the algorithm's sorting of them. For example, when a *Schitt's Creek* fan comes across a Moira Rose cosplay video, they might comment "Commenting so I can stay on SchittTok," thus simultaneously publicly proclaiming their love for the television series and telling the algorithm what type of content they want to see. Ruehlicke adds, "being properly recognized by the algorithm is presented as a sign of having found your community."[24] By the same token, TikTokers also tell the algorithm which communities they *don't* belong to. For instance, when I see content that I don't want to see, I typically swipe up as fast as I can so the algorithm recognizes that I didn't engage with the post more than I had to. By avoiding content that we don't like, TikTokers are also teaching the algorithm. Belonging to certain TikTok subcultures means not belonging to others.

Given that TikTok is known for virality, not only do videos and TikTokers go viral, but these identity blueprints and cultures also go viral, a phenomenon that is marked, as scholar José van Dijck notes, by content "spill[ing] over into social platforms and mainstream media."[25] Many avid TikTok scholars, journalists, and users believe that TikTok's algorithm makes the prospect of going viral significantly more likely than on rival social media platforms.[26] The result is a user base that buys into the dream of TikTok fame, pouring time, energy, and money into creating high-quality and entertaining content that will draw attention on the app and beyond. Viral content accumulates millions of views on the platform before entering an afterlife on other media and Web 2.0 spaces. This explains why viral TikTok content dominates meme culture on social media sites such as Facebook, Instagram, and Twitter. As TikTok's virality extends further and further away from the platform itself, TikTok becomes more ingrained in culture. It begins to dictate the way we self-fashion our identities, live our day-to-day lives, interact with other people, and so on and so forth.

In *Perpetual Motion: Dance, Digital Cultures, and the Common*, dance scholar Harmony Bench understands dance in digital cultures as a phenomenon marked by repetition in which users "have co-ownership in the creation of a dance experience."[27] Although Bench is speaking explicitly of dance in the digital realm, her thoughts apply to how TikTok virality creates a sense of co-ownership that, in turn, creates community. That is, by engaging in TikTok trends, we all take ownership in them, canonizing them and cementing their place in popular culture. Ownership, therefore, is how TikTok becomes culture. And, repetition is how it stays that way. Bench notes, "Repetition makes-common by making an idea, gesture, or style familiar."[28] When TikTokers mimic one another, recreating trending challenges, they facilitate the "proliferation and extended life" of that challenge.[29] TikTokers also make challenges their own, which influences and contributes to the culture as well. As the phenomenon repeats itself, TikTok becomes more and more synonymous with offline cultures. This is why when we hear Doja Cat's "Say So" or Megan Thee Stallion's "Savage" in the car, at a club, or at a high school dance, we inevitably perform the corresponding dance challenge made famous by TikTok. Performing these viral dance moves signals a place of belonging in group culture as much as it does personal identity formation. We perform these dances while wearing clothing that TikTok has told us are fashionable. As we talk to our friends over the lyrics, we use slang made popular by TikTok. And, we capture the entire experience in a vlog-style TikTok video showcasing just how memorable the experience was. TikTok, for these reasons, is everywhere. For many of us, TikTok is our culture. There's no denying that.

Chapter Organization

This book is divided into three sections, each focusing on TikTok's relationship to US popular culture. The first section, Race and Ethnicity on TikTok, considers the increasingly complicated relationship between TikTok and communities of color in the United States. Despite the praise that TikTok has received from the media, scholars, and app users, the app has also had several noteworthy missteps. For example, the app is known as a site for racism and violence toward communities of color. Chapters in this section consider how TikTok reinforces whiteness, how the app engages in digital eugenics, and how racism proliferates on the app. Chapters ask: How do the TikTok algorithm and shadowbanning work to suppress content by creators of color, queer creators, and disabled creators? How do Digital Blackface and Antisemitism operate within TikTok? How can marginalized communities thrive on TikTok while also battling white supremacy on the app? How do whiteness and, by extension, white supremacy operate on TikTok? And, despite anti-Blackness and xenophobia on TikTok, how can the platform also be a space of joy and Black/Latinx excellence?

In Chapter 1, Trevor Boffone theorizes the "D'Amelio Effect" to encompass how the cultural production of white teenage stars such as Charli D'Amelio influences the cultural actions of millions of US teens. Next, Cienna Davis proposes that the uneven rewards for white performers on TikTok constitute a form of digital Blackface minstrelsy that troubles Gen Z's supposed racial progressivism. In Chapter 3, Wendyliz Martinez questions how Black girls resist narratives of exploitation and create a space of joy and self-care on TikTok. Next, Tom Divon and Tobias Ebbrecht-Hartmann focus on the emerging #JewishTikTok community, which transforms TikTok into an affinity space to communicate Judaism.

The book's second section, Gender and Sexuality on TikTok, frames TikTok as a space to build inclusive feminist and queer communities. Offering theoretical models from youth studies, feminist theory, and queer theory, these chapters serve as blueprints for future scholarly engagement with the platform's cultural trendsetters—girls/women and queer people. Chapters question: What roles do gender and sexuality play on TikTok? How does girlhood materialize on TikTok? In what ways can TikTok be a space of intergenerational feminist community-building? How do LGBTQ+ TikTokers queer the app? Why do queer folks flock to TikTok? What does queer community look like on the platform?

The section begins with Shauna Pomerantz and Miriam Field, who unpack their notion of "radical media engagement" in which TikTok facilitates an intergenerational, multidirectional feminist learning. Claudia Skinner, in Chapter 6, explores how queer women and nonbinary creators use TikTok as a site of queer world-making through which they craft cultural texts and produce digital resources to build queer communities. The section concludes with Chapter 7 in which Elle Rochford and Zachary D. Palmer examine how trans TikTokers explore, depict, and negotiate trans identity on the app.

The third section, TikTok (Sub)Cultures, highlights how identities and, by extension, communities are formed on TikTok. The app's notorious algorithm sorts users into various thriving subcultures. These chapters trace connections and genealogies between TikTok subcultures and other social media apps that predate TikTok. Chapters ask: How are communities formed on TikTok? How do community norms and values emerge, if at all? How does TikTok work as an affinity space? What is the role of TikTok subcultures within the app's larger mainstream culture? How do TikTok cultures expand into nondigital spaces? How are TikTok subcultures different than ones on social networks such as Facebook, Twitter, and Instagram?

In Chapter 8, Jane Barnette focuses on the community of users who tag their videos with a combination of WitchTok and "spells" (or #WitchTokSpells), with the goal of sharing themselves casting a spell. In Chapter 9, Katlin Marisol Sweeney-Romero surveys how Wellness TikTokers advertise an aspirational, "aesthetic" self-image on their profile known as "that girl": a professionally successful figure whose accomplishments extend to her curated social media presence and uniform self-presentation. Elena Machado Sáez, in the book's final chapter, identifies key trends in how US Latinx theaters use TikTok, while discussing the potential and limits of these survival strategies.

The book concludes with an afterword by Frederick Luis Aldama which considers how TikTok lies at the avantgarde of pop culture. Synthesizing many of this collection's most salient arguments, Aldama encourages us to recognize the positives and negatives of TikTok while also seeing how the space can become a "transculturative and transformative creative critical collaboratory."

Notes

1 D. Bondy Valdovinos Kaye, Xu Chen, and Jing Zeng, "The Co-Evolution of Two Chinese Mobile Short Video Apps: Parallel Platformization of Douyin and TikTok," *Mobile Media & Communications* 9, no. 2 (2020): 229–253.

2 Jing Zeng, Crystal Abidin, and Mike S. Schäfer, "Research Perspectives on TikTok and Its Legacy Apps," *International Journal of Communication* 15 (2021): 3162.

3 For more on the growth of TikTok as well as discussions about the app's interface and features, see Crystal Abidin, "Mapping Internet Celebrity on TikTok: Exploring Attention Economies and Visibility Labours," *Cultural Science Journal* 12, no. 1 (2021): 77–103; Kaye, Chen, and Zeng, "The Co-Evolution of Two Chinese Mobile Short Video Apps."; Andreas Schellewald, "Communicative Forms on TikTok: Perspectives from Digital Ethnography," *International Journal of Communication* 15 (2021): 1437–1457; and Zeng, Abidin, and Schäfer, "Research Perspectives on TikTok and Its Legacy Apps."

4 TikTok now allows selected users the opportunity to upload videos up to three minutes long. These videos are few and far between on the app. Shorter content reigns supreme.

5 In addition, there are several forthcoming books on TikTok in 2022. For example, Bondy Valdovinos Kaye, Jing Zeng, and Patrik Wikstrom's, *TikTok: Creativity and Culture in Short Video* (Cambridge: Polity Press, 2022) examines TikTok's platform features while also considering the sociocultural implications of TikTok. Crystal Abidin's, *TikTok and Youth Cultures* (Bingley: Emerald, 2022) focuses on TikTok in the Asia Pacific region, paying close attention to how youth are central to TikTok's success.

6 Raymond Williams, *Culture* (London: Fontana Press, 1981), 200.

7 "TikTok made me do it" challenges see TikTokers trying out new foods, fashions, tourist locations, etc. TikTokers use the app to leave a vlog-style review.

8 John Koetsier, "Digital Crack Cocaine: The Science behind TikTok's Success," *Forbes*, January 18, 2020, https://www.forbes.com/sites/john koetsier/2020/01/18/digital-crack-cocaine-the-science-behind-tiktoks-success/?sh=31d4f56e78be.

9 Jing Zeng, Crystal Abidin, and Mike S. Schäfer, "Research Perspectives on TikTok and Its Legacy Apps," *International Journal of Communication* 15 (2021): 3163.

10 Wallaroo Media, "TikTok Statistics–Updated June 2021," June 14, 2021, https://wallaroomedia.com/blog/social-media/tiktok-statistics/.

11 Generation Z pertains to those born roughly between 1997 and 2015.

12 Andreas Schellewald, "Communicative Forms on TikTok: Perspectives from Digital Ethnography," *International Journal of Communication* 15 (2021): 1439.

13 Trevor Boffone, *Renegades: Digital Dance Cultures from Dubsmash to TikTok* (New York: Oxford University Press, 2021), 6.

14 Karl Spracklen, *Digital Leisure, the Internet and Popular Culture* (London: Routledge, 2015).

15 For more on how digital leisure spaces become spaces of public pedagogy, see Emma Rich and Andy Miah, "Understanding Digital Health as Public Pedagogy: A Critical Framework," *Societies* 4 (2014): 296–315.

16 danah boyd, *It's Complicated: The Social Lives of Networked Teens* (New Haven, CT: Yale University Press, 2014), 6.

17 Kyesha Jennings, "City Girls, Hot Girls and the Re-Imagining of Black Women in Hip Hop and Digital Spaces," *Global Hip Hop Studies* 1, no. 1 (2020): 49.

18 Deanna Ting, "'Every Kid Wants to Be an Influencer': Why TikTok Is Taking Off with Gen Z," *Digiday*, February 7, 2020, https://digiday.com/marketing/every-kid-wants-influencer-tiktok-taking-off-gen-z/.

19 Howard Gardner and Katie Davis, *The App Generation: How Today's Youth Navigate Identity, Intimacy, and Imagination in a Digital World* (New Haven, CT: Yale University Press, 2013), 32.

20 Ibid., 121.

21 Andrea Ruehlicke, "Just for You: TikTok and Personalization," *Flow Journal* 27, no. 1 (2020), https://www.flowjournal.org/2020/10/content-just-for-you/.

22 Kirsten Drotner, "Leisure Is Hard Work: Digital Practices and Future Competences," in *Youth, Identity, and Digital Media*, ed. David Buckingham (Cambridge, MA: MIT Press, 2008), 170.

23 Ruehlicke, "Just for You."

24 Ibid.

25 José van Dijck, *The Culture of Connectivity: A Critical History of Social Media* (London: Oxford University Press, 2013), 77.

26 Maria Sibirtseva, "Insightful Tips on TikTok Marketing to Reach Generation Z and Millennials," *Deposit Photos*, August 4, 2020, https://blog.depositphotos.com/tips-on-tiktok-marketing.html.

27 Harmony Bench, *Perpetual Motion: Dance, Digital Cultures, and the Common* (Minneapolis: University of Minnesota Press, 2020), 3.

28 Ibid., 21.

29 Ibid., 21–22.

Section One

Race and Ethnicity on TikTok

1 The D'Amelio Effect

TikTok, Charli D'Amelio, and the Construction of Whiteness

Trevor Boffone

In September 2020, Dunkin Donuts released a much-publicized new menu item—The Charli. The drink, named after TikTok's most-followed creator, Charli D'Amelio, combines cold brew, whole milk, and three pumps of caramel syrup. Oh, and you can't modify the drink. If you want to order The Charli, you have to get it just as D'Amelio orders her favorite drink. D'Amelio's videos frequently include her drinking iced coffee, making her collaboration with Dunkin an organic choice, while also speaking to the crossover success of TikTok stars such as D'Amelio, who got "TikTok Famous" for hitting dance challenges in their bathrooms and bedrooms before becoming veritable celebrities in the United States in 2020.

I saw The Charli on TikTok and immediately got in my car. I'm not a Charli D'Amelio fan; I don't follow her. But my FOMO crept in. I didn't want to miss out. I had to know what the hype was about. Within one sip, I knew the drink was too sweet for me. At least I tried it once.

A week later, I had to try it again.

"Can I get The Charli with one less pump of caramel?"

"No, we can't modify The Charli."

It appeared, if I wanted to belong to this exclusive club, then I had to drink The Charli as is, in all of its sugary goodness.

How did I end up at Dunkin? A 34-year-old man influenced to buy a drink that a 16-year-old was advertising on TikTok. By this point, the tremendous marketing potential of TikTok was starting to become more apparent, but to me, what stood out was how I had engaged with what I call the "D'Amelio Effect." As Charli D'Amelio goes, so does TikTok. And as TikTok goes, so does US (popular) culture.

By this point in fall 2020, the United States was firmly entrenched in a youthquake, a term that media studies scholar Bill Osgerby uses to "describe the more general impact young people and their cultures

DOI: 10.4324/9781003280705-3

have had, since the early twentieth century, on patterns of social, economic, and political change around the world."[1] The youthquake in question? TikTok. Young people, as always, are "a driving force in 'seismic' social change,"[2] and the age of TikTok has been no different. Whereas popular Gen Z social media apps such as Instagram, Snapchat, Houseparty, and YikYak have all been fundamental sites for contemporary teenager identity formation, their cultural impact has often been relegated to those platforms. In contrast, as the chapters in this volume collectively attest, TikTok culture is culture culture; it penetrates mainstream culture in the United States. And, while many casual observers will quickly dismiss TikTok as a silly app for teens and bored adults, there is more to the platform than meets the eye. Tik-Tok has changed the way we create, consume, and interact with digital media. And, given the United States' legacy of white supremacy, Tik-Tok in this country is far from immune to critiques of whiteness. Even the vignette about iced coffee that began this chapter doesn't appear to conjure notions of whiteness and systemic white supremacy. But, upon further inspection, we find whiteness at its root. Whiteness is pervasive. Whiteness is there.

This chapter examines the power of TikTok's top tier of influencers, including not just Charli D'Amelio, but other young women like Addison Rae, and young men including Bryce Hall and Noah Beck. Although many scholars focus on popularity, virality, and fame on TikTok, the platform is not without its criticisms, many of which revolve around how whiteness operates within and outside of the space. Building off research in my first book, *Renegades: Digital Dance Cultures from Dubsmash to TikTok*, I use the "D'Amelio Effect" to encompass how the cultural production of teenage stars such as Charli D'Amelio influences the cultural actions of millions of teens (and adults) in the United States. As TikTok's most-followed account, with over 136 million followers, D'Amelio has an unparalleled level of influence and, as a result, dictates the culture of the app, including trending challenges, songs, and dances, not to mention her broader societal influence as a brand ambassador for companies such as Dunkin Donuts. Yet, the "D'Amelio Effect" is not without complications. It both dictates mainstream TikTok culture and reinforces whiteness on the app, perpetuating systems of racism and white supremacy that exist offline. While TikTok may be an escapist digital paradise for many, it is very much part of the real world and, as such, has a lasting influence on how whiteness is constructed in the United States in the TikTok age. In *Whiteness Fractured*, Cynthia Levine-Rasky asks, "How is whiteness done?"[3] I ask, how is whiteness done on TikTok?

TikTok Celebrity and the Rise of the D'Amelio Effect

On March 10, 2020, Charli D'Amelio appeared on *The Tonight Show Starring Jimmy Fallon*. She inaugurated a new skit on the show in which a famous TikToker teaches Fallon new TikTok dances.[4] At this point, just ahead of the US shutdown in the wake of COVID-19, TikTok was still largely the realm of teenagers. TikTok mystified most adults, who dismissed TikTok (youth) culture entirely or didn't care. It wasn't until weeks later that TikTok would explode in the country, leaving many adults suddenly wanting to consume all things TikTok. On Fallon, D'Amelio offered a glimpse into how far her celebrity status had come from her debut on the app just one year before, when she found sudden virality on the way to dance camp, almost immediately becoming the app's most followed account and resident "it" girl. D'Amelio became famous for posting her signature dance videos, which millions of TikTokers mimicked, remixed, and "dueted" (recording their own clip side by side with hers). By March 2020, D'Amelio was one of the most visible examples of TikTok fame. Although my work here focuses on D'Amelio, a host of influential teenagers and young 20-somethings, including Addison Rae, Loren Gray, Dixie D'Amelio, Lil Huddy, Noah Beck, and Bryce Hall (I could go on) gained clout, or social media fame and power, in 2019 as TikTok became one of the most important spaces for youth culture. Notably, these TikTok influencers are all white or white-passing, thus reinforcing the racial power dynamics of TikTok. While the app can be an inclusive, democratized space, TikTok fame mirrors general fame in the United States, which privileges whiteness and conventional Western beauty standards.

Social media fame is not unique to TikTok. Social media scholar Crystal Abidin recognizes that social media platforms give rise to prolific users, who, in turn, become the platform's celebrities: "they are often the leaders of trends within subcultures, and perhaps even the highest earners through brand collaborations and ad sales."[5] In *Internet Celebrity: Understanding Fame Online*, Abidin affirms that the central aspect of celebrities on social media platforms is their high visibility.[6] Figures such as D'Amelio might begin their celebrity on TikTok, but their fame spills out far beyond the reaches of social media, cementing them as celebrities whose presence and influence go far beyond what users see and interact with on the app. Although D'Amelio's TikTok bio once read, "don't worry i don't get the hype either,"[7] by March 2020, she had already made the aforementioned guest appearance on *The Tonight Show*, appeared at the 2020 NBA All-Star Game, filmed a 2020 Super Bowl commercial with Jennifer Lopez, and amassed high-profile corporate sponsors. Her book, *Essentially Charli: The Ultimate Guide to Keeping It Real* (2020), became a *New York Times* bestseller as soon as it hit shelves, proving that TikTok fame does, in fact, translate to marketing power.

Media studies scholar Melanie Kennedy recognizes how "many of the most-followed stars of TikTok are not only young, but female, normatively feminine, white and wealthy."[8] When we think of girlhood on TikTok, users like D'Amelio are the default. When my Black students show me videos of new dances that they want to teach me, they are often videos of D'Amelio or other young women who fit into the D'Amelio aesthetic ("slim, white, normatively attractive").[9] This power dynamic is baked into the app itself. TikTok videos are not sorted chronologically, for example. Rather, when users search a hashtag or sound bite, TikTok shows the results in batches, with the most viewed videos appearing at the top. Given that the majority of the platform's mega stars are white, these videos often feature white creators, in many cases suggesting that these creators have choreographed these dances or initiated these trends. Thus, the platform's racial power dynamics continue, spilling out into the analog world in which my Black students want to learn dances that Charli D'Amelio supposedly creates. But, of course, in many cases, D'Amelio did not create these dances. In fact, TikTok dance crazes are largely created by Black teenagers who rarely reap the rewards of initiating a viral TikTok trend.

I use the "D'Amelio Effect" to embody the tremendous power that TikTok famous stars like Charli D'Amelio hold to influence the app's mainstream culture as well as mainstream US culture in general.[10] Although the term borrows D'Amelio's name, it is not limited to just her. Rather, the D'Amelio Effect can be applied to how Loren Gray or Addison Rae, for example, shape TikTok culture, generational Zoomer culture, and, more increasingly, popular culture in the United States. What many dismissed as digital child's play before the pandemic has transformed into an incredible amount of mainstream influence that is often held by young white women, even as they mimic the work of Black teens, continuing a legacy of cultural appropriation and white people profiting off the work of Black people.

Writing for *Forbes*, John Koetsier calls TikTok content "digital crack cocaine."[11] If that is so, then replicating Charli D'Amelio is how we get our fix. We watch her dance videos on loop, learning her moves while exponentially growing her engagement rate. As we try to sync our bodies perfectly with D'Amelio's, we are telling the TikTok algorithm that this is exactly the type of content that we want to see and that others like us want to see, as well. We want to move like her. We want to dress like her. We'll even spend money on a too-sweet iced coffee drink just because it has her name. Media studies scholar Andreas Schellewald describes TikTok videos "not as random and short-lived entertainment but as complex, cultural artifacts."[12] When TikTokers make meaning via mimicking or engaging with D'Amelio, inevitably they are making meaning that is imbued in whiteness. That is, something as seemingly irrelevant as Charli D'Amelio dancing to "Renegade (Lottery)" by K Camp or "Twerkulator" by City Girls is in fact part of a system that promotes whiteness while obfuscating Blackness and the cultural contributions of the Black artists who sing these songs and the Black dancers who choreograph the corresponding dance challenges—challenges that are reenacted by D'Amelio before penetrating the app's mainstream culture and, from there, US culture at large.

TikTok Is a White Space

In April 2021, I visited my family in New Orleans. As had become commonplace in my family since the dawn of TikTok, I made TikToks with my eight-year-old niece Charlie. While Charlie and I had ideas for the dance, I decided to ask my Instagram followers for dance challenges that they wanted us to hit. The results quickly started to come in. One stood out: Twerkulator. I immediately searched the name on TikTok. Per usual, the first video to pop up was none other than Charli D'Amelio. I clicked on the video. D'Amelio was in her bathroom, clad in a sheer black top and jeans, and sporting braided pigtails. She danced to "Twerkulator" by City Girls. If this had taken place a year earlier, I might have mistakenly believed that D'Amelio had choreographed the Twerkulator Challenge. In 2021, though, D'Amelio left no doubt who created the dance—Layla Muhammad.[13] As had become customary in the post-Renegade TikTok era, D'Amelio gave dance credit, or "dc." In this case, the millions of viewers on the video could easily click on Muhammad's handle (@layzchipz), bringing them to the challenge's creator and alleviating any doubt about who began this popular TikTok trend.

Despite D'Amelio calling back to Muhammad and working to properly credit Black artists, the TikTok platform inevitably elevates creators like D'Amelio, who have dozens of millions more followers than any creator of color on the app. That is, when someone searches for "Twerkulator," TikTok elevates the likes of D'Amelio far higher than the Layla Muhammads, Jalaiah Harmons, Mya Nicole Johnsons, and

Dl Nayahs of the digital dance world.[14] Even when D'Amelio attempts to right the ship, whiteness becomes the default, with the app's algorithm resorting back to whiteness and thus becoming another tool of white supremacy. Although blatant racism does take place on TikTok, the app's white supremacist culture goes beyond explicit anti-Black behaviors. In *Whiteness Fractured*, Cynthia Levine-Rasky notes that whiteness "is primarily about the exercise of power, often practiced subtly or obliquely, but always with the effect of its construction—and exclusion—of difference."[15] On TikTok, white supremacist culture is subtle, operating so smoothly that most users will never even realize that it exists.

TikTok exemplifies how digital platforms often reinforce white supremacy and further social inequality, which media studies scholars Safiya Umoja Noble and Ruha Benjamin propose is a signature of new technologies that claim to be inclusive, oppressive-free spaces.[16] TikTok is designed to uphold whiteness as not just the norm, but as something aspirational. At its roots, as much as TikTokers may criticize D'Amelio, we want what she has—clout, access, followers, fame, you name it. We aspire to have what she has. As a white supremacist structure, the D'Amelio Effect is rooted in both the individual and the system. The process begins when D'Amelio uploads a video to TikTok. Regardless of whether she has created the dance or has mimicked the work of another creator, D'Amelio's actions initiate trends on the app, beginning on her page and spreading like wildfire. While her personal decisions appear to be precisely that—personal—they, in fact "reinforce the social, political, economic, and other privileges that white people have."[17] Although racism and white supremacy are institutions that go far beyond the individual, "part of the way that these institutions are able to so effectively privilege white people and exploit non-white people is through the development of individual attachments and commitments to them."[18] In the world of TikTok, someone like D'Amelio can be aware of the system, but as long as she continues to invest in it, the system will not change. For example, when the issue of cultural appropriation and dance credit on TikTok reemerged in January 2020 surrounding the Renegade Dance Challenge, D'Amelio addressed the issue head on, apologizing for her oversight and collaborating with Jalaiah Harmon. D'Amelio began to give dance credit on her videos, thus modeling the practice for her millions of followers. Later, at the height of the George Floyd protests, D'Amelio uploaded a video in which she named police brutality and systemic anti-Blackness directly. But, even as this white teen learns about her white privilege and the ways in which she benefits from anti-Blackness, D'Amelio continues to benefit from these institutions precisely because she is white. As the saying goes, "all white people are racist since they benefit from racism." Regardless of her interventions, D'Amelio will continue to be overvalued on spaces like TikTok because she exemplifies the pinnacle of Gen Z culture in the United States.

The D'Amelio Effect is rooted in TikTok's challenge culture, which relies on recreating dances and trends, sometimes adding unique spins to them to set the video apart, and at other times perfectly mimicking the video. Anoop Nayak recognizes that "whiteness is produced, consumed, regulated, adapted, and transgressed in [our] lives," "conveyed through repetition, stylized gestures, parodic reiterations, and corporeal enactments that purport that these racial inscriptions are somehow 'real.'"[19] Sara Ahmed affirms,

> Whiteness 'holds' through habit. Public spaces take shape through the habitual actions of bodies.... We need to examine not only how bodies become white, or fail to do so, but also how spaces can take on the very 'qualities' that are given to such bodies.[20]

This aligns with TikTok's challenge culture. TikTok is built around TikTokers mimicking the platform's most-followed accounts. That is, the repetition and virality of D'Amelio's videos, trends, dances, and aesthetics replicate whiteness. While D'Amelio's celebrity grows, so, too, does the reach and uses of whiteness on TikTok. As Ahmed suggests, whiteness is reproduced because it is "seen as a form of positive residence."[21] That is, whiteness is comforting. It feels normal. It feels safe. It feels like home. On TikTok in the United States, Charli D'Amelio is the mainstream. Charli D'Amelio appearing on a user's FYP (For You Page) is normal, reminding TikTokers of who holds power in this digital space. D'Amelio feels like home.

If, as Osgerby recognizes, youth are "active agents in culture consumption and creation,"[22] then making and engaging with TikTok is a form of agency. Or, as danah boyd proposes, teens use social media to "write themselves and their community into being."[23] But, what happens when that agency is tied to other groups losing agency? And, what happens when some communities are canonized as the TikTok mainstream, whereas others are not? Levine-Rasky notes how racism is "relational." That is, not only does racism affect racialized groups, it is also conceptualized in terms of "the affirmation, advantage, and power it conveys to white groups."[24] Whiteness is marked by entitlement and exclusion.[25] On the one hand, white TikTok stars are entitled to opportunities that Black TikTokers are excluded from. Even in the case of *The Tonight Show Starring Jimmy Fallon*, when social media backlash criticized Addison Rae and Fallon in March 2021 for not giving credit to Black creators (a year after D'Amelio had gone on the show and done the same thing), the Black creators were later featured on the show in a purely digital way. None of them were flown to New York to dance with Fallon at Studio 6B at 30 Rockefeller Center. Their experience was, in fact, a watered-down version of Addison Rae's *The Tonight Show* debut.

This racial power dynamic is relational. When teens like D'Amelio gain power through TikTok, they do not simply gain power from a vacuum. Rather, they attain power precisely because other communities lose power. Even if TikTokers of color, too, gain agency and power via TikTok, inevitably the platform's white supremacist structure amplifies the agency of white teens, thus recreating centuries of anti-Blackness and white supremacy in wholly new, supposedly inclusive space. In this case, D'Amelio has power precisely because Jalaiah Harmon doesn't. Although Harmon's Renegade growth launched her career, her social and cultural mobility paled in comparison to D'Amelio's lucrative deals and march toward 136 million followers (and growing). Systems of white supremacy give Black teens such as Jalaiah Harmon just enough opportunity so that the system can say that the system doesn't exist. But while Jalaiah Harmon, Mya Nicole Johnson, Chris Cotter, and Keara Wilson have gotten their due, Black artists like D1 Nayah and others whose dances have been performed on *The Tonight Show Starring Jimmy Fallon* have not.[26]

Of course, the D'Amelio Effect is not all positive for the young women who embody it. Charli D'Amelio—like others including Addison Rae and Jojo Siwa—has been subject to misogyny. And, of course, this conversation is not limited to women. Take, for instance, a common genre of videos in which TikTokers duet content by Bryce Hall, Noah Beck, and company. TikTokers make fun of the boys, mocking how they think people react to their videos. These videos are often hilarious, but further inspection reveals that TikTokers inevitably like Hall and Beck. They have millions of followers and all of the perks that come from TikTok fame.[27] Although it's easy to criticize them and recognize their lack of talent and conventional hotness, on TikTok, these boys are the norm. The term "TikTok Boys" conjures images of white boys with perfectly chiseled bodies and conventional Western beauty standards of hotness. Even as we make fun of them, we want what they have. We want to be TikTok boys. That is, their power and position on the social hierarchy exists precisely because we are *not* them. On TikTok, whiteness is often subtle. Even content by people of color can play into how the app reinforces and privileges whiteness. Operating under the table is how it perseveres. With each duet, people of color make fun of Bryce Hall, for example, while also giving him more TikTok power by sharing the original video, linking to his profile, and, perhaps, most relevant, maintaining the conversation's focus on Bryce Hall rather than on creators of color. TikTok, therefore, exploits creators of color on the platform in service of promoting white content creators.

Conclusion

Of course, many people disregard the racial politics of TikTok. When controversies arise on TikTok and Instagram, the comments sections swell with many social media users writing that "it's *just* TikTok. It's not that serious." As Kyra Gaunt recognizes, most young TikTokers dismiss the cultural context of TikTok content, especially digital Blackface and jokes relating to anti-Blackness. Gaunt notes, "The whole system is about gamifying our humiliation, laughter, embarrassment, shame, crying…. It's all about monetizing and gaming that stuff for attention. But there is no critical reflection, downtime."[28] When videos of D'Amelio circulate and her followers recreate "her" dances, the cultural context of these dances is lost. That is, as the #RenegadeChallenge exploded in late fall 2020, for example, the context of the dance's origins and the anti-Blackness baked into its popularity were lost on the majority of TikTokers. Meanwhile, D'Amelio's celebrity skyrocketed as the dance she supposedly created became arguably TikTok's most famous dance challenge in the platform's short history. Thus works the D'Amelio Effect.

As D'Amelio goes, so, too, does TikTok. So, too, does Gen Z and, increasingly, US popular culture. As TikTok stars like D'Amelio continue to experience a meteoric rise, we must continue to be critical of TikTok as a white supremacist system, even if we are implicated in how whiteness proliferates on and off the app. Whiteness, as always, is ubiquitous in the United States. TikTok is no exception.

Notes

1 Bill Osgerby, *Youth Culture and the Media: Global Perspectives* (Oxfordshire: Routledge, 2021), 1.
2 Osgerby, 1.
3 Cynthia Levine-Rasky, *Whiteness Fractured* (Oxfordshire: Ashgate, 2013), 14.
4 On March 26, 2021, fellow TikToker Addison Rae would also appear on *The Tonight Show.* Both appearances highlighted how the work of Black creators is obfuscated on TikTok in favor of privileging white creators.

5 Crystal Abidin, "Mapping Internet Celebrity on TikTok: Exploring Attention Economies and Visibility Labours," *Cultural Science Journal* 12, no. 1 (2021): 79.
6 Crystal Abidin, *Internet Celebrity: Understanding Fame Online* (Bingley: Emerald, 2018).
7 Jamilah King, "TikTok's Charli D'Amelio Talks Surviving Internet Fame," *Teen Vogue*, February 17, 2021, https://www.teenvogue.com/story/charli-damelio-young-hollywood-2021.
8 Melanie Kennedy, "'If the Rise of the TikTok Dance and E-Girl Aesthetic Has Taught Us Anything It's That Teenage Girls Rule the Internet Right Now': TikTok Celebrity, Girls and the Coronavirus Crisis," *European Journal of Cultural Studies* 23, no. 6 (2020): 1071.
9 Kennedy, 1072.
10 Trevor Boffone, *Renegades: Digital Dance Cultures from Dubsmash to TikTok* (New York: Oxford University Press, 2021), 2.
11 John Koetsier, "Digital Crack Cocaine: The Science Behind TikTok's Success," January 18, 2020, https://www.forbes.com/sites/johnkoetsier/2020/01/18/digital-crack-cocaine-the-science-behind-tiktoks-success/.
12 Andreas Schellewald, "Communicative Forms on TikTok: Perspectives from Digital Ethnography," *International Journal of Communication* 15 (2021): 1439.
13 For more on TikTok and the issue of dance credit, see Boffone, *Renegades*.
14 Jalaiah Harmon is widely known as the creator of the Renegade Challenge. Mya Nicole Johnson received widespread notoriety for choreographing with Chris Cotter the viral dance to "Up" by Cardi B. D1 Nayah is colloquially known as "The CEO of Viral Dances," notably creating the Donut Shop Challenge. For more on these creators and dance challenge culture, see Boffone, *Renegades*.
15 Levine-Rasky, 12.
16 Safiya Umoja Noble, *Algorithms of Oppression: How Search Engines Reinforce Racism* (New York: New York University Press, 2018); Ruha Benjamin, *Race after Technology: Abolitionist Tools for the New Jim Code* (Boston, MA: Polity Press, 2019).
17 Shannon Sullivan, *Revealing Whiteness: The Unconscious Habits of Racial Privilege* (Bloomington: Indiana University Press, 2006), 4.
18 Sullivan, 4.
19 Anoop Nayak, *Race, Place and Globalization Race, Place and Globalization Youth Cultures in a Changing World* (New York: Berg, 2003), 173.
20 Sara Ahmed, "A Phenomenology of Whiteness," *Feminist Theory* 8, no. 2 (2007): 156.
21 Ahmed, 154.
22 Osgerby, 126.
23 danah boyd, "Why Youth [Heart] Social Network Sites: The Role of Networked Publics in Teenage Social Life," in *Youth, Identity, and Digital Media*, ed. David Buckingham (Cambridge, MA: MIT Press, 2008), 120.
24 Levine-Rasky, 23.
25 David Theo Goldberg, "The Social Formation of Racist Discourse," in *The Anatomy of Racism*, ed. David Theo Goldberg (Minneapolis: University of Minnesota Press, 1990), 307.

26 Keara Wilson is the creator of the viral dance to "Savage" by Megan Thee Stallion.

27 As of November 2021, Noah Beck has 31 million followers and Bryce Hall has 21 million followers.

28 Tatiana Walk-Morris, "TikTok's Digital Blackface Problem," Medium, February 12, 2020, https://onezero.medium.com/tiktoks-digital-blackface-problem-409571589a8

2 Digital Blackface and the Troubling Intimacies of TikTok Dance Challenges

Cienna Davis

One day before the WHO declared the coronavirus a global pandemic, 19-year-old Keara Wilson[1] turned to TikTok to alleviate her boredom. Within an hour, she had created and uploaded 15 seconds of original choreography to the new single "Savage" by Houston rapper Megan Thee Stallion onto TikTok.[2] In the early days of the pandemic, people of all backgrounds swayed their hips, rolled their backs, and tauntingly stuck out their tongues to Wilson's original choreography. The dance spread rapidly until Megan herself was performing Wilson's choreography online and on-stage. In a matter of days, #SavageChallenge became one of the first viral dance challenge of the pandemic amassing billions of views on TikTok.

At face value, Wilson's story reflects the rhetoric that has made TikTok Gen Z's app of choice: the possibility for any bored teen to go viral from their bedroom. And dance, as the de facto language of mainstream TikTok, has become a reliable method for virality on the app.[3] But, in reality, Wilson posted her choreography five times to TikTok before it was catapulted to virality by TikTok's most famous influencer, Charli D'Amelio (128 M followers).[4] D'Amelio, whose infamous popularization of Jalaiah Harmon's 2019 Renegade dance marked an important shift in the culture of crediting on TikTok after early failures of adopters to tag the creator, posted videos performing (and tagging) Wilson's choreography for three days in a row. D'Amelio accumulated over 30 M likes with the dance.[5] The "D'Amelio Effect" aligned with the digital marketing campaign for Megan's new album that (urged by TikTok) put their sponsorship money into "Savage."[6] Predictably, the #SavageChallenge blew up serving as a vehicle for the album and D'Amelio's continued success. Like many other Black girls creating dances on TikTok and Dubsmash, Wilson (3.2 M followers) enjoyed relatively modest success from the challenge while the greatest rewards were reserved for Megan, D'Amelio, and mega-influencer

DOI: 10.4324/9781003280705-4

Addison Rae (85 M followers) who was invited to perform the dance on *The Tonight Show Starring Jimmy Fallon*. The so-called #Black-TikTokStrike of July 2021, following the release of Megan's latest single "Thot Shit," demonstrates a tonal shift from "petty grievances" of kids online to a verifiable labor issue where money, attention, and opportunities are expropriated from Black creators.[7]

From Vine and Twitter to Dubsmash and TikTok, many of the most popular digital trends emerge from the local practices of Black youth who continuously innovate online.[8] Though it is not often framed as tech innovation, dance challenges are one such space where we see the games that Black girls play to perform and articulate their racial, gender, and sexual identities driving technocultural trends and undermining the default Whiteness and masculine bias of virtual space.[9] TikTok's misleading rhetoric of democratizing the attention economy invites users from all backgrounds to the platform by obscuring the algorithmic, economic, and ideological mechanisms at work that elevate certain users and trends in the service of TikTok's goals of accumulating capital, sustaining user attention, facilitating brand deals, securing creator loyalty, and tightening their grip on the music and culture industries altogether.[10] While young Black women like Wilson are creating defining cultural moments with original choreography, within TikTok's digital attention economy, it is Black femme[11] rhythms, gestures, and affect that emerge as a dark mine of commercial and social profit for white influencers.[12]

During the pandemic, dance challenges offered a playful escape for isolated young Americans of all backgrounds to connect. But the uneven rewards for white influencers performing Black dances within TikTok's attention economy implicitly signals what Jason Parham refers to as an "evolution of digital blackface."[13] On TikTok, this evolution is characterized by predatory inclusion, whereby misleading rhetoric of democratizing the attention economy invites Black creators to their supposedly egalitarian platform on extractive terms, as well as cultural extraction, where Black digital innovation, play, and creativity become fungible, or *commodities to freely exchange*, within the digital attention economy.[14] Rather than reaping the full social and economic rewards of their content, Black creators are repeatedly alienated from the product of their labor without proper credit and compensation. Instead, their labor and play become a source of commercial profit for platforms and white influencers who are miscredited with creating cultural trends.[15] This chapter ultimately questions what it would mean for the viral content of Black creators on TikTok to be regarded instead as a non-fungible commodity, whose ownership is unique, clear, irreplaceable, and compensated.

Dance challenges thus offer a complex site to examine the intersecting racial and gender dynamics of platform capitalism within today's most ascendant social media platform. Placing dance challenges within the broader historical context of blackface minstrelsy and connecting it to Jasmine E. Johnson's notion of flesh dance, I argue that the uneven rewards for white performers on TikTok constitutes a discreet yet insidious form of digital blackface minstrelsy that troubles the contours of Gen Z's supposed racial progressivism. To evaluate the cross-racial intimacies that can trouble dance challenges, I offer a scale for assessing participation from playful exchange to cultural extraction. I then conclude by considering how platforms and influencers might undermine this exploitative digital economy through justice-oriented investments.

Gen Z and Performative Allyship

Myths of American post-racialism and colorblindness that pervaded the Obama presidency dissolved with the subsequent 2016 election of Donald J. Trump. But mass Gen Z mobilization for gun control, against climate change, and in defense of Black lives offered a visual foil to the conservatism of Trump's base. Despite the diversity and progressivism that has characterized Gen Z, racial segregation in the United States continues to be re-enforced at a structural (housing, schools, employment) and interpersonal level, leaving meaningful interracial interactions in the United States at surprising lows.[16]

As the exchange of language for social justice becomes more widespread online but meaningful interracial interactions remain at a surprising low for young people offline, performative allyship flourishes. Like the black squares that flooded social media on June 2, 2020 (i.e. #BlackoutTuesday)[17] as a purported symbol of support for Black Lives Matter, performative allyship publicly gestures toward allegiance to a cause for social justice from a nonmarginalized group without demonstrating substantive action to alleviate the suffering and discrimination of the oppressed group. When activism is trending, performative allyship replaces actual sacrifice, personal responsibility, and accountability from the beneficiaries of oppressive systems.[18]

During the summer's racial uprisings, many praised D'Amelio for speaking out against the killing of George Floyd and changing her profile picture to "Black Lives Matter." These symbolic gestures, however, do nothing to rectify her own complicity in the systems of cultural extraction and racial capitalism that exploits Black labor in her dance-related content. While it's challenging to assess one's private contributions, I will later provide examples of how mega-influencers like D'Amelio and Rae can lead the way by moving beyond symbolic gestures and crediting toward demonstrating substantive steps to undermine the extractive economies they profit from.

Digital Blackface and Flesh Dance

Blackface minstrelsy is one of the earliest performance traditions in US history. From theater and film to the comic and music industry, white racial fantasies of the Black body have engendered a racially exploitative economy within the American entertainment industry. Though the painting of white skin brown for laughs and commercial entertainment faces widespread censure today, blackface minstrelsy adapts to the social and material relations of the times ensuring cultural extraction under subtler forms. Observing the transformation of blackface minstrelsy over time thus offers valuable insights into the maintenance of racial capitalism within the media system.

Digital blackface minstrelsy signifies the various ways that the Internet and digital technologies facilitate parodic performances of the Black racial other. Earlier writing on digital blackface by Amanda Hess, Lauren Michelle Jackson, and Ellen E. Jones critiqued the overuse of Internet GIFs and memes featuring Black people by non-Black users on image and text-based social media platforms like Twitter, Facebook, Tumblr, and Instagram.[19] These memes perform heightened emotions, evoke humor, and appropriate Black vernacular for non-Black users seeking to garner the cultural capital associated with Black expressivity, or the "vibrancy, intensity, unsurpassed joy in living" that oft characterizes Black subjectivities under the constant threat of extermination or captivity.[20] The technological move toward video-based apps like TikTok where users mime and lip-sync audio memes has transformed the more passive sharing of racial affect into a participatory form of digital minstrelsy that has heightened its political impact through embodiment and expropriation of Black cultural expression.[21]

The study of blackface minstrelsy has traditionally focused on white men performing exaggerated stereotypes of black masculinity and rascality, but digital blackface increasingly relies upon the cultural desire to mimic and appropriate Black feminine expression.[22] The contributions of Black masculinities to digital culture (including dance culture) cannot be underestimated, but the disturbing trend of embodied appropriations of Black feminine expression serving as an accelerant for virality remains under examined.[23]

Our cultural comfort with the mimicry and exploitation of Black women traces back to the legacy of chattel slavery. Hortense Spillers clarifies how the physical and discursive violence enacted upon enslaved Black women transformed her body into maimed flesh, branding her as a commodity of capitalist exchange, a means of reproducing free, laboring slave property. The enslaved Black woman was thus marked as "a receptable for others' desires, fears, and capitalist ambitions."[24] Over time, the discursive maintenance of this maiming has relied upon the concretization of racist and sexist caricatures or "controlling images" of hypersexuality that overdetermine sociohistorical understandings of the racially and sexually marked Black female body.[25] Black women's bodies have thus served as vehicles for capitalist accumulation through physical labor, reproductive labor, and the libidinal economy tied to her sexualized flesh. Despite the strides made by Black women in American society, the historical notions bound to her captive flesh reemerge as justification for the exploitation and violence enacted upon her.

Within hip-hop culture, Black women's bodies have traditionally been objectified and relegated to the role of the "video vixen," a reiteration of the classic Jezebel stereotype of the "hypersexual" Black woman.[26] Jasmine Johnson aptly offers the term "flesh dance" to evoke the proprietary legacy permeating the libidinal dance of Black female-identified bodies as they suggestively move to hip-hop lyrics.[27] The legacy of Black women's sexual exploitation does not disclose the pleasure Black femmes derive from modest or immodest dance. Across the diaspora, the rhythmic shaking of one's flesh exudes collective and agential joy, pride, sensuality, skill, and creativity. But the term flesh dance nonetheless points to a longstanding economy of extraction and fungibility that exploits "the vulnerability of the captive body as a vessel for the uses, thoughts, and feelings of others."[28]

Famous for her raunchy, skillful lyricism and voluptuous curves, Megan Thee Stallion is one figure whose music has been at the center of various TikTok trends, including various ultra-popular dance challenges.[29] Dance challenges and the evolution of digital blackface have created avenues for a new cadre of Black women rappers such as Flo Milli, Doja Cat, and the City Girls who have historically been excluded from masculinist economies of hip-hop to be agents and profiteers of their racialized and sexualized bodies. Megan's digital marketing campaigns benefit from dance challenges, flesh dance, and the eagerness of white women to exploit the fungibility, or malleability, of the Black femme body as a vessel for their own desires.

In "Eating the Other," bell hooks writes that

> [w]hen race and ethnicity become commodified as resources for pleasure, the culture of specific groups, as well as the bodies of individuals, can be seen as constituting an alternative playground where members of dominating races, genders, sexual practices affirm their power-over in intimate relations with the Other.[30]

Thinking of platforms like TikTok as virtual playgrounds for Gen Z, dance challenges constitute a networked dancefloor for social play. The intimacies of cross-racial play are, however, troubled by legacies of exploitation recreated in digital space. The embodiment of Black feminine bodily gestures and affect across the Internet commercially benefits the platform and facilitates meaning-making processes that serve the interests and desires of individual users, able to laud their own digital interfacing with Black culture and more intimately with the Black femme body outside of context. Drawing upon Johnson, I argue that the mimicry of Black femme flesh dance should not be confused with legibility or intimacy with the interiority of Black women (and by virtue their demands for justice) but rather reinscribes proprietary relations of domination that enforce Black women's precarity in American society.[31]

From Playful Exchange to Cultural Extraction

The popularity of dance challenges illustrates that mimicry of Black cultural expression remains a viable rite of passage for white youth. It is, however, important to note that there is no singularly negative way to interpret participation in dance challenges. Participation is welcomed by all and does not necessarily equate to exploitation when performed by the outgroup. And yet, the troubling intimacies between white youth and Black femme bodies within this practice demands recognition and self-awareness from those in the outgroup who participate. For this reason, I have developed a scale for scholars to evaluate the exploitative nature of digital dance cultures they encounter online, from playful exchange to cultural extraction.

1 Mimicry as youth identity formation and community building
    Digital space is increasingly the avenue where Gen Z articulates their identities and builds community. Dance challenges online provide such space for youth to cultivate meaningful social intimacies and express one's identity. On less mainstream

video-sharing apps like Dubsmash with a more ethical culture of crediting, Trevor Boffone's 2021 book *Renegades* demonstrates how personal growth and community building for many youth online exceeds the desire for virality, clout, and followers.[32] This demonstrates how the ideological priorities of a platform and its algorithm structure its extractive character.

2   Mimicry as "self (as other) parody"[33]

This category makes a joke of the creator's inability to embody the style and sensuality of the source choreography. Such parody often involves white family members participating in dances challenges, like user @hey.brittanyyy who teaches her father Wilson's dance. Usually just a playful cultural exchange or impersonation, the category enters troubling territory when the success and humor rely upon overemphasizing difference from a racial "other." User @chillchillchillchill's parody of #SavageChallenge and #BodyChallenge (see footnote 29) with his "uncoordinated" family catapults engagement on his page from the low thousands to nearing a million likes and millions of views. While Wilson had to post multiple videos of her choreography for her talent to be recognized and gain traction, white users lacking coordination can build followings with greater ease by dipping into the profitable well of racial parody.

3   Mimicry as sexualization/adultification (flesh dance)

A popular category of mimicry is that of scantily clad femmes using the challenge to assert their sexuality. Reliance on the supposedly unbridled sexuality of the Black female body to perform one's maturity and edge reinforces the dangerous adultification of Black girls. Compared to their white peers, reports show that Black girls are disproportionately perceived as being less feminine, more aggressive, and less deserving of the traditional protections of youth and femininity.[34] The use of dance challenges to assert one's sexuality as the member of an outgroup safe from these dangerous stigmatizations contributes to a culture of implicit bias that leaves Black children vulnerable to harm, like that of 16-year-old Ma'Khia Bryant, a young Black girl and TikToker, who was shot and killed by police outside of her foster home during a crisis.[35]

4   Mimicry as capital/attention accumulation

This category addresses mega-influencers like D'Amelio and Rae described throughout this chapter who use dance challenges to accumulate attention and capital, often through sponsorships requiring a specific amount of engagement on their videos. Their massive reach makes these deals the obvious choice, but when the influencer relies upon the intellectual property of another creator who is not financially compensated by the influencer or sponsor, these represent the heights of cultural extraction.

Conclusion

On July 29, 2021, over a year after #SavageChallenge went viral, Wilson, along with five other BIPOC creators (supported by the JaQuel Knight Foundation and Logitech), celebrated copyright victories that formally recognized their choreographies as intellectual property.[36] These landmark victories ensure credit and compensation when their choreography is featured in films, commercials, or video games. It remains to be seen how this development will impact the attention, opportunities, and income of these creators, but this victory demonstrates the ingenuity and determination of Black creators to be recognized for their work while also meaningfully undercutting the fungibility of Black intellectual property on TikTok, hopefully creating new pathways for other creators.

With Blackness treated as a fungible commodity from which to extract value, what would it mean for the viral content of Black creators on TikTok to be regarded as non-fungible? Non-fungibility would mean that the value of the content cannot be transferred to others without consent and compensation of the creator. Although the current hype around the market for non-fungible tokens (NFT)[37] resembles a playground for the ultra-rich and is unlikely to target racial injustice in the arts and entertainment, the concept of an NFT is a compelling one for creators from marginalized communities whose work has been so readily expropriated within the US entertainment industry.[38] If TikTok would like to meaningfully address the labor concerns of Black creators whose work is so often extracted of value, they should broker deals between influencers and sponsors that regard the source from which the influencer draws as non-fungible. With wealthy white influencers earning multi-million-dollar incomes in a year, those whose content mimics or appropriates the content of lesser-known Black creators can be allies by demonstrating their willingness to share a portion of their relevant profit. Or they can be content with relying on their own creativity.

Notes

1 Keara Wilson's TikTok username is @keke.janajah.
2 Megan Uy, "An Interview with Keara Wilson, the 19-Year-Old Dancer Behind the 'Savage' TikTok Choreo," *Cosmopolitan*, August 5, 2020, https://www.cosmopolitan.com/lifestyle/a33471157/keara-wilson-tiktok-savage-dance-creator/.

3 Rebecca Jennings, "The Most Popular Dances Now Come from TikTok. What Happens to Their Creators?" *Vox*, February 4, 2020, https://www.vox.com/the-goods/2020/2/4/21112444/renegade-tiktok-song-dance.
4 All follower and like counts from December 2021.
5 Taylor Lorenz, "The Original Renegade," *The New York Times*, July 16, 2020, sec. Style, https://www.nytimes.com/2020/02/13/style/the-original-renegade.html.
6 Trevor Boffone, *Renegades: Digital Dance Cultures from Dubsmash to TikTok* (New York: Oxford University Press, 2021), 2.
7 Taylor Lorenz and Laura Zornosa, "Are Black Creators Really on 'Strike' from TikTok?" *The New York Times*, June 25, 2021, sec. Style, https://www.nytimes.com/2021/06/25/style/black-tiktok-strike.html; Kari Paul, "'They Can't Do It without Us': Black TikTokers Strike to Protest Dance Appropriation," *The Guardian*, June 24, 2021, http://www.theguardian.com/technology/2021/jun/24/tiktok-strike-black-creators-megan-thee-stallion-dance.
8 A recent study from the University of Chicago even shows that Black teens create more content online than any other racial group. Cathy Cohen et al., "Participatory Politics: New Media and Youth Political Action," Youth & Participatory Politics, June 2012, https://ypp.dmlcentral.net/publications/107.html.
9 Kyra Danielle Gaunt, *The Games Black Girls Play: Learning the Ropes from Double-Dutch to Hip-Hop* (New York: New York University Press, 2006); Kishonna L. Gray, "Race, Gender, and Virtual Inequality: Exploring the Liberatory Potential of Black Cyberfeminist Theory," in *Produsing Theory in a Digital World 2.0: The Intersection of Audiences and Production in Contemporary Theory* (New York: Peter Lang, 2015), 185.
10 Shelly Banjo, "TikTok Part 3: 'I'll Be Making Bank! Hopefully.,'" mp3, Foundering, accessed May 5, 2021, https://podcasts.apple.com/us/podcast/tiktok-part-3-ill-be-making-bank-hopefully/id1161880916?i=1000519176079.
11 I use the term "femme" to engage the ways that femininity is not confined to one fixed binary gender. Black femmes may fluidly identify with and perform femininity. The embrace of femininity and feminine forms of expression is not limited to cis-women, but includes those who are queer, non-binary, and gay.
12 Jason Parham, "TikTok and the Evolution of Digital Blackface," *Wired*, August 4, 2020, https://www.wired.com/story/tiktok-evolution-digital-blackface.
13 Ibid.
14 Tressie McMillan Cottom, "Where Platform Capitalism and Racial Capitalism Meet: The Sociology of Race and Racism in the Digital Society," *Sociology of Race and Ethnicity* 6, no. 4 (October 1, 2020): 445, https://doi.org/10.1177/2332649220949473.
15 Kalhan Rosenblatt, "Months after TikTok Apologized to Black Creators, Many Say Little Has Changed," *NBC News*, February 9, 2021, https://www.nbcnews.com/pop-culture/pop-culture-news/months-after-tiktok-apologized-black-creators-many-say-little-has-n1256726; Trevor Boffone, "Jimmy Fallon, Addison Rae, and the Issue of TikTok Dance Credit," *The Theatre Times*, April 2, 2021, https://thetheatretimes.com/jimmy-fallon-addison-rae-and-the-issue-of-tiktok-dance-credit/; Paul, "'They Can't Do It without Us.'"

16 Lisa Cannell, "Segregation in 2020: Why Aren't We Moving Forward?," *Darden Ideas to Action*, September 1, 2020, https://ideas.darden.virginia.edu/segregation-in-2020.

17 During the racial uprisings of summer 2020, Blackout Tuesday began as an initiative to draw attention to the racial injustices within the music industry. Individuals would post a black square to their social media feed with #TheShowMustBePaused and were expected to challenge racism within their organizations. It was quickly adopted by users across the Internet under #BlackLivesMatter. While it could be said to signal a popular discursive shift in support for Black Lives Matter (which in previous years was a controversial statement), it also disrupted more useful sharing within the hashtag and prioritized symbolic over substantive support for the movement.

18 Holiday Phillips, "Performative Allyship Is Deadly (Here's What to Do Instead)," *Medium* (blog), June 4, 2020, https://forge.medium.com/performative-allyship-is-deadly-c900645d9f1f; McKenna Kelley, "Performative Activism Is Basically Silence. Here's Why.," *SWAAY*, June 15, 2020, https://swaay.com/performative-activism-silence-protest-allyship.

19 Amanda Hess, "The White Internet's Love Affair With Digital Blackface," *New York Times*, 2017, https://go-gale-com.proxy.library.upenn.edu/ps/i.do?p=BIC&u=upenn_main&id=GALE%7CCCT521271184&v=2.1&it=r&sid=summon; Lauren Michele Jackson, "We Need to Talk About Digital Blackface in GIFs," *Teen Vogue*, August 2, 2017, https://www.teenvogue.com/story/digital-blackface-reaction-gifs; Ellen E. Jones, "Why Are Memes of Black People Reacting so Popular Online?" *The Guardian (London, England)*, July 8, 2018, Gale OneFile: News, https://link.gale.com/apps/doc/A545823058/STND?u=upenn_main&sid=STND&xid=485520c6.

20 bell hooks, "Eating the Other: Desire and Resistance," in *Black Looks: Race and Representation* (Boston, MA: South End Press, 1992), 35.

21 Danielle Robinson, "Performing American: Ragtime Dancing as Participatory Minstrelsy," *Dance Chronicle* 32, no. 1 (2009): 113; Crystal Abidin, "Mapping Internet Celebrity on TikTok: Exploring Attention Economies and Visibility Labours," *Cultural Science Journal* 12, no. 1 (January 19, 2021): 80, https://doi.org/10.5334/csci.140.

22 Joshua Lumpkin Green, "Digital Blackface: The Repackaging of the Black Masculine Image," (Oxford, OH: Miami University, 2006); Miles White, *From Jim Crow to Jay-Z: Race, Rap, and the Performance of Masculinity* (Baltimore, MD: University of Illinois Press, 2011), http://ebookcentral.proquest.com/lib/upenn-ebooks/detail.action?docID=3413906; Douglas A. Jr. Jones, "Black Politics But Not Black People: Rethinking the Social and 'Racial' History of Early Minstrelsy," *TDR: The Drama Review* 57, no. 2 (2013): 21–37.

23 Hess, "The White Internet's Love Affair with Digital Blackface"; Jackson, "We Need to Talk About Digital Blackface in GIFs"; Jones, "Why Are Memes of Black People Reacting so Popular Online?"; Parham, "Evolution of Digital Blackface."

24 Jasmine Johnson, "Flesh Dance: Black Women from Behind," in *Futures of Dance Studies*, eds. Susan Manning, Janice Ross, and Rebecca Schneider (Madison: University of Wisconsin Press, 2020), 152, 158, http://muse.jhu.edu/book/71575; Hortense Spillers, "Mama's Baby, Papa's Maybe: An American Grammar Book," *Diacritics* 17, no. 2 (1987): 64–81.

25 Patricia Hill Collins, *Black Feminist Thought: Knowledge, Consciousness, and the Politics of Empowerment*, 2nd ed. (New York: Routledge, 2009), https://www.routledge.com/Black-Feminist-Thought-Knowledge-Consciousness-and-the-Politics-of-Empowerment/Hill-Collins/p/book/9780415964722.
26 Collins; Tricia Rose, *The Hip Hop Wars: What We Talk about When We Talk about Hip Hop—and Why It Matters*, November 2, 2008 (New York: Civitas Books, 2008).
27 Johnson, "Flesh Dance," 157.
28 Saidiya V. Hartman, *Scenes of Subjection: Terror, Slavery, and Self-Making in Nineteenth-Century America*, Race and American Culture (New York: Oxford University Press, 1997), 19, https://catalog.hathitrust.org/Record/003949065.
29 #SavageChallenge, #SavageRemix, #CaptainHookChallenge, #Body-Challenge, #WAPChallenge
30 hooks, "Eating the Other," 23.
31 Johnson, "Flesh Dance," 158.
32 Boffone, *Renegades*, 9–13.
33 Robinson, "Performing American."
34 Rebecca Epstein, Jamilia Blake, and Thalia González, "Girlhood Interrupted: The Erasure of Black Girls' Childhood," SSRN Scholarly Paper (Rochester, NY: Social Science Research Network, June 27, 2017), https://doi.org/10.2139/ssrn.3000695.
35 Kiara Alfonseca, "Ma'Khia Bryant Case Shines Light on 'adultification' of Black Girls," *ABC News*, May 14, 2021, https://abcnews.go.com/US/makhia-bryant-case-shines-light-adultification-black-girls/story?id=77427522.
36 Audrey Tang, "Logitech and Visionary Choreographer JaQuel Knight Drive Change for BIPOC Creators through Copyright Protection and New Film," *Business Wire*, July 29, 2021, https://www.businesswire.com/news/home/20210729005677/en/Logitech-and-Visionary-Choreographer-JaQuel-Knight-Drive-Change-For-BIPOC-Creators-Through-Copyright-Protection-and-New-Film.
37 Non-fungible tokens enable the trade of unique digital items, such as animated GIFs, memes, or other digital art that are tracked on a digital ledger known as blockchain. Cryptocurrency investors have been known to spend millions on a single NFT, but the longevity of the NFT market remains to be seen.
38 Mitchell Clark, "People Are Spending Millions on NFTs. What? Why?," *The Verge*, March 3, 2021, https://www.theverge.com/22310188/nft-explainer-what-is-blockchain-crypto-art-faq.

3 TikTok for Us by Us

Black Girlhood, Joy, and Self-care

Wendyliz Martinez

In April 2021, Ma'Khia Bryant's TikTok videos circulated the internet to honor her life after she was fatally shot by a police officer.[1] This phenomenon differed from prior cases of police brutality in which explicit videos of Black people being brutalized or killed have been circulated. In the case of Bryant, the officer's body cam footage was released and shown on the news, but in online spaces, people refused to circulate this violent video. Instead, users on online spaces such as Facebook and Instagram wanted to depict Bryant during moments of joy. These videos show how Ma'Khia Bryant created a space for herself virtually that enabled her to have fun and express joy. In Bryant's TikTok videos featuring her having fun doing her hair, her joyous expressions radiate through the screen. Using Bryant's TikToks as a point of departure, this chapter focuses on how Black girls use TikTok as a site to express and find joy online, a critical component of privileging self-care habits.

This chapter is an extension of my ongoing research on Black and (Black) Latinx girls between the ages of 12 and 18 and their social media habits. Here, I focus on how Black girls have used TikTok to express Black joy and how TikTok has evolved in their lives since the COVID-19 pandemic. While there are many studies that provide research on both the negative and positive effects social media has on adolescence,[2] including the ways adolescents develop social identity, I write about the ways that Black girls have constructed spaces for themselves in positive ways. Black joy is an act of resistance. As such, I explore how Black girls on TikTok exemplify joy and, as an extension, *resist*. Resist what exactly? Since this chapter started as a survey about the COVID-19 pandemic, I observe the ways that Black girls resist capitalist narratives that require them to be productive. At the beginning of the COVID-19 pandemic, there was a push for people to be creative and productive with this "newfound time" from having to stay indoors. This mindset completely

DOI: 10.4324/9781003280705-5

overlooked how many essential workers and students still had to work even if it was from home. Just because most people were in lockdown did not mean they had free time. Therefore, I first questioned the ways that girls resisted the narrative of productivity but it evolved into much more as TikTok's popularity has only increased since March 2020.

In what follows, I concentrate on two interviews I conducted with Siah (16) and Lee (13), who are from New York City, as well as close readings of the way Ma'Khia Bryant's videos were circulated online after her murder.[3] I engage with Audre Lorde's ideas of self-preservation from her text *A Burst of Light* and bell hooks' "Homespace," two theoretical tools that can to speak to how Black girls position self-care, illness, and safe-spaces as central to finding joy and thriving on TikTok. Self-preservation in the face of oppression is a skill. This chapter questions: How do Black girls exemplify joy on TikTok? How do Black girls practice self-care on TikTok?

Self-preservation and Homespace

As TikTok has grown in popularity, scholars such as Melanie Kennedy, Crystal Abidin, and Trevor Boffone have been attuned to how girlhood is experienced on the platform. For example, Kennedy focuses on TikTok as a site of girls' bedroom culture with a particular focus on Charli D'Amelio. While TikTok celebrates girlhood, there are still potential harms of creating celebrity culture around teenage girls. Abidin extends this research, focusing on celebrity and influencer culture on TikTok as well as its attention economy. Boffone's work explores how Black girls are TikTok's trendsetters, work that is often culturally appropriated and exploited by white creators.[4]

My research adds to this scholarship by focusing on how Black girls resist both capitalistic productive narratives and online celebrity culture. Furthermore, I expand on extant literature in Black Girlhood Studies by scholars such as LaKisha Simmons, Aria A. Halliday, and Ashleigh Wade, as well as Black Feminist scholarship that critiques capitalism by scholar Francis M. Beal. Simmons' work gives scholars a way to understand age as a category of analysis and apply that analysis to the ways Black girls navigated violence from the Jim Crow South while adhering to their middle class expectations of respectability. Halliday provides scholars a way to understand the way that Black girls contribute to embodied knowledge as well as "collective Black girl pleasure."[5] Wade demonstrates how Black girls form digital kinships through social media and how digital spaces can provide possibilities for Black girls to seek support and grow networks.[6] Beal analyzes the intersections of oppression specifically for Black women and critiques capitalism.[7] My work builds on this scholarship by considering how age, embodied knowledge, and capitalism all contribute to the ways Black girls interact with TikTok and engage in activities they deem as self-care.

Considering the extant scholarship, I return to the question of how Black girls exemplify joy and practice self-care online. To answer this, I use hooks' notion of "homespace." For hooks, Black women have resisted the white supremist capitalist narratives through the "homespace." hooks defines homespace as such:

> This task of making a homespace... was about the construction of a safe place where black people could affirm one another and by so doing heal many of the wounds inflicted by racist domination.... in that "homespace," most often created and kept by black women,... we had the opportunity to grow and develop, to nurture our spirits.[8]

hooks emphasizes how the "homespace" is a "safe space" where folks can "grow" and, most relevant to this chapter, "nurture our spirits." There are many obstacles that attempt to dehumanize Black girls. Therefore, it is important for these girls to "nurture the spirit." For the girls that I interviewed, TikTok becomes a "homespace" where they can nurture their spirits.

I put the concept of "homespace" in conversation with Lorde's ideas about self-preservation as resistance because of how these concepts complement each other. However, as Beal writes,

> The system of capitalism (and its afterbirth...racism) under which we all live, has attempted by many devious ways and means to destroy the humanity of all people, and particularly the humanity of black people. This has meant an outrageous assault on every black man, woman, and child who resides in the United States.[9]

Given that capitalism denies bodily autonomy to Black girls, self-care becomes an act of political resistance, not unlike how Black joy is an act of resistance. Speaking then to self-preservation, Lorde writes, "Caring for myself is not self-indulgence, it is self-preservation, and that is an act of political warfare." She also states,

> I wish to live whatever life I have as fully and as sweetly as possible, rather than refocus that life solely upon extending it for some unspecified time. I consider this a political decision as well as a life-saving one...[10]

Lorde famously wrote these words when she was battling cancer, effectively stating that caring for herself is not just political but also "life-saving." Both hooks and Lorde in these works write about the importance of taking care of oneself and community which emphasizes the harmony between the concepts of "homespace" and self-care. These two things are connected because the preservation of a Black body goes against capitalism's intent—which is to destroy. Likewise, for these Black girls participating in activities that go against "productivity" (mostly schoolwork and other similar responsibilities) is not just making a political decision (to go against an education system not always made for them), they are making a self-preserving one.

In light of hooks' and Lorde's assertations, young Black girls resist by doing pleasurable things and taking care of their bodies. As mentioned previously, I collected ten surveys during the start of the COVID-19 pandemic, where more than half of the girls revealed that they enjoyed doing things such as baking, painting, drawing, and fewer said they enjoyed watching Netflix. These glimpses into what brings these girls joy demonstrate the things that girls were excited to do, especially during a time that was marked by uncertainty and isolation. Each of these activities goes beyond the stereotypical idea of what teenagers today like to do: spend countless hours on their iPad playing on social media and watching YouTube. The girls I surveyed preferred doing things that didn't involve technology, except for TikTok which was frequently emphasized for its "funness." The fact that these girls cited TikTok as a site to have fun returns to hooks' idea of "homespace." From these interviews, I assert that TikTok becomes a "homespace" for these girls after they cultivate a specific way to engage with the platform. These girls are aware of the ways that capitalism has tainted social interactions on social media, mainly people trying to go viral.

The Interviews

Here, I focus on interviews with Siah and Lee since both girls provided insight into TikTok, paying close attention to how adolescent girls interact with the social media platform. Siah and Lee had similar ways of creating a "homespace" for themselves on TikTok and practiced similar tactics in ways that can be interpreted as self-care. Both girls centered fun around how they engaged with the platform. The original survey was distributed among my networks, where I asked people to share with girls between the ages of 10 and 18. I interviewed girls that provided more detailed answers in these surveys and because I knew their parents personally, which facilitated setting up the interviews, which were a mix of in person and video chat. I was able to interview Siah and Lee twice. For these two girls, they viewed fun as the guiding factor of engaging with TikTok. Lee and Siah identify as Black Latina and Black, respectively, and both live in New York City in different boroughs but attend public school. The girls emphasize the For You Page (FYP) and how TikTok can be a different experience depending on the person's FYP. They also understand that there are algorithms in place that tailor these videos based on the kinds of videos you watch. By liking and interacting with videos, they believed they can mold their FYPs to privilege humorous and entertaining content. This is part of creating a homespace, playing with the algorithm so that the algorithm feeds these girls videos that they find entertaining. In this way, these girls regain some sort of agency over the algorithm.

Furthermore, both girls signal how celebrity, or rather influencer culture, can potentially taint the homespace. In corresponding to influencer culture, Lee reveals how young girls are surveilled. In her interview, she told me the "history" of TikTok and how it was Musical.ly first.[11] She was excited about knowing this history and that she was a part of Musical.ly, and eventually TikTok before it became mainstream. She also believes that Musical.ly was more positive than when the app was dissolved into TikTok. She believes that with the "mainstream" came negativity such as users being more judgmental and engaging in cancel culture. Therefore, users need to be "careful" with the kinds of content they produce lest they be canceled because of it, as she stated. However, Lee's advice only applies to those with public profiles, which she did not have since hers is private. In keeping with influencer culture, Siah recognizes how many users can get discouraged because of their desire to be similar to/become influencers and go viral. Yet, Siah recognizes that on TikTok it is easier to gain viral content as opposed to other platforms. She mentioned, "If you want to become famous all you have to do is be consistent on TikTok." Both Lee and Siah emphasize the nature of how people are under surveillance by having public profiles which could potentially be positive (if you want to be an influencer), but oftentimes creates room for negativity due to either disappointment or bullying.

Additionally, regarding surveillance, Lee's father checks what she posts to make sure it is "appropriate." There are many ways to interpret this. She must succumb to respectability politics of what is appropriate while the idea of visibility (and in some sense virality) lies in the background. She claims she only makes videos she knows her parents will approve of. But despite her agency over her own video creation, her parents eventually stopped allowing her to be on the app because of the content that began appearing on her feed. Lee understands that the content she puts out can be separated from her as a person. She highlights cancel culture and the ways that sometimes content can be misunderstood and cause others to "cancel" you. She added that content can be used for "bashing" or bullying. If you do a dance wrong, or even if you try too hard can cause bullying or being canceled according to her. Content on a site like TikTok has the possibility to become a disembodied representation of you and therefore can be appropriated and reinterpreted. As seen through the appropriation of Black creators' content, TikToks can have a public life of their own, disengaged from the creator themself. However, the way that both girls resisted is "simple" as far as a solution. Both girls had their pages private, which enables only their followers to view their content. This prevented their content from reaching people they did not know or allow on their page. Lee would post dance videos and lip-synching videos, but Siah mentioned that she didn't post often. In fact, she would go back and delete her posts after a while because she did not like being visible online, even to her curated followers. She preferred to browse and swipe through the FYP. In this case, both girls created their homespace, protected it, and participated in self-preservation by not being interested in being "public," therefore limiting any negative backlash from the content they posted.

The girls' responses emphasize the quotidian nature of TikTok, meaning it's for regular people and to have fun, not to do anything "extra." For example, when celebrities use it in a way that defeats the purpose of TikTok (such as having better camera quality or professional style dancing). Prior to the COVID-19 pandemic, TikTok was mainly used by Gen Z, where low-quality/simple videos were uploaded, such as the videos that Lee would post that featured her lip-synching. The rise of actual celebrities and "professionalization" on TikTok since COVID-19 has changed the landscape of TikTok. However, as Abidin's research reveals, this does not fully change that the preferred content on TikTok is more quotidian style videos.

The girls spoke about how they have used TikTok. They send videos to friends through text as a form of video "memes," they would try to make videos performing the dances and post them privately, and they sometimes just saved the video in their drafts and would later delete it. Again, these actions speak to the ways that they are using these apps for themselves and are not interested in outside gazes. They use TikTok to make sense of their lives by finding funny videos that relate to something they went through or are developing knowledge about themselves through embodiment and performing. This corresponds to Halliday's work on how the body can serve as a learning site, how it becomes a "repository of knowledge," to understand oneself and history.[12] These girls practice this knowledge production by performing popular dances. Each of these girls' bodies is policed by society and sometimes even their families in different ways which they subvert by posting videos privately.

Conclusion

I now return to Ma'Khia Bryant. Bryant's death at the hands of police adds to the exhausting list of Black people murdered by the nation state. Yet, recent online discourse has brought awareness to the ways that the humanity of the victims has been denied through the sharing of violent videos of their deaths. With Bryant, the circulation of her TikTok videos was a response to the ways that victims of police brutality have their final moments shared recklessly. Contrary to the body cam footage, in the TikTok videos, Bryant is seen doing her hair, using a familiar style of editing that is popular on the site. She is also seen lip-synching in videos and doing hand choreography. These videos are reminiscent of the type of videos that are often uploaded by Gen Z creators and the previously popular format of TikTok videos as mentioned by Siah and Lee. Bryant created her homespace, where she did her hair, smiled, sang, and danced. While her page was public, she shared her videos for her enjoyment. Her TikTok is still active with a bio edited to state, "Love live my sister #makhiabryant JUSTICE FOR MAKHIA BRYANT." The reaction to Bryant's death and subsequent videos being shared felt different than the response to Breonna Taylor's death. Taylor was almost turned into a celebrity figure, even being featured on a magazine cover. This sensationalism also did not seem "better" than the circulation of violent videos either. She was refashioned into what could be described as an influencer where her images seemed to be disconnected from her humanity. In contrast, the circulation of Bryant's TikToks was a moment of resistance to that idea of celebrity. Her TikTok videos showed her as a "regular" young girl who liked to have fun online. We resisted the narrative of her being a "dangerous" youth, a person that deserved their fate. She is preserved in a moment of time where she is happy. Her image continues to exist within her homespace where she is safe from projection of others, reminiscent of the bio's words "love live."

I end with what we learn from these three girls and their contributions through their content whether it is visible or decidedly invisible.

As Lorde mentions, these girls are living their life as sweetly as possible, not focused on the negative aspects that they navigate often but just in the present. Whether it's the fun of learning a new TikTok dance or sharing their hair care routine, we learn to continue doing what we enjoy despite fear, because if we succumbed to fear, then we wouldn't do anything.

Notes

1 Nicholas Bogel-Burroughs, Ellen Barry, and Will Wright. "Ma'Khia Bryant's Journey Through Foster Care Ended with an Officer's Bullet," *The New York Times*, May 8, 2021, accessed August 1, 2021, https://www.nytimes.com/2021/05/08/us/columbus-makhia-bryant-foster-care.html
2 Walaa Elsayed, "The Negative Effects of Social Media on the Social Identity of Adolescents from the Perspective of Social Work," *Heliyon* 7, no. 2 (February 21, 2021), https://doi.org/10.1016/j.heliyon.2021.e06327.
    "How Using Social Media Affects Teenagers," Child Mind Institute, August 16, 2021, https://childmind.org/article/how-using-social-media-affects-teenagers/.
3 Ma'Khia Bryant's TikTok handle is @makhia03.
4 Melanie Kennedy, "'If the Rise of the TikTok Dance and e-Girl Aesthetic Has Taught Us Anything, It's That Teenage Girls Rule the Internet Right Now': TikTok Celebrity, Girls and the Coronavirus Crisis," *European Journal of Cultural Studies* 23, no. 6 (2020): 1069–1076; Crystal Abidin, "Mapping Internet Celebrity on TikTok: Exploring Attention Economies and Visibility Labours," *Cultural Science Journal* 12, no. 1 (2021): 77–103; and Trevor Boffone, *Renegades: Digital Dance Cultures from Dubsmash to TikTok* (New York: Oxford University Press, 2021).
5 Aria S. Halliday, "Twerk Sumn!: Theorizing Black Girl Epistemology in the Body," *Cultural Studies* 34, no. 6 (2020): 1–18.
6 Ashleigh Wade, "When Social Media Yields More Than 'Likes': Black Girls' Digital Kinship Formations," *Women, Gender, and Families of Color* 7, no. 1 (2019): 80–97.
7 Frances M. Beal, "Double Jeopardy: To Be Black and Female," *Meridians* 8, no. 2 (2008): 166–176.
8 Bell Hooks, *Yearning: Race, Gender, and Cultural Politics* (Boston, MA: South End Press, 1990).
9 Beal "Double Jeopardy," 166.
10 Audre Lorde, *A Burst of Light: Essays* (Ithaca, NY: Firebrand Books, 1988).
11 Musical.ly was a lip-syncing app released in 2014. Musical.ly was acquired by ByteDance in 2017 and merged with TikTok in 2018.
12 Halliday, "Twerk Sumn!"

4 #JewishTikTok

The JewToks' Fight against Antisemitism

Tom Divon and Tobias Ebbrecht-Hartmann

"Hitler was right!" This frequently seen comment exemplifies the toxic environment that Jewish TikTokers (self-professed "JewToks") have faced in the age of TikTok. Shadowed by the increase in hate speech on social media since the Trump presidency, antisemitism toward Jewish communities in the United States has penetrated TikTok. "Ever since I joined TikTok and recognized myself as a Jew, I received antisemitic comments daily, regardless of the content," one JewTok explained in an interview for this chapter. For her, as for hundreds of Jewish creators, TikTok has become an echo chamber where hateful ideas circulate and sinister content flourishes.

In response, a squad of Jewish-American TikTokers have decided to cleanse the digital atmosphere and dedicate their accounts to combatting antisemitism. Our chapter introduces four leading TikTokers who identify as part of the emerging #JewishTikTok community in the United States, transforming TikTok into an affinity space to communicate about and educate on Judaism. Examining the subculture's infrastructure on the platform, we first elaborate on two significant threats to Jewish creators' visibility: (1) TikTok's dark side that pushes users to "memeify" antisemitism utilizing the platform's trends and aesthetics; (2) TikTok's algorithmic repression, in which the platform's moderation system tends to block JewToks' responses to antisemitic content.

This vicious cycle leads Jewish creators into performative strategies, which we analyze to unpack the dialogic modes of communication involved. Based on interviews with creators and close analysis of their strategies, we explore their unique ways of combating antisemitism by translating Jewish concepts into TikTok's vernacular. By being attentive to trends and harnessing #JewishTikTok, a hashtag with over 650 M views, creators grant access to their subculture's burning issues. Among others, they combat Holocaust denial while

DOI: 10.4324/9781003280705-6

dancing and lip-syncing in challenges, destigmatize Jewish culture using the respond-to-comments feature, immerse themselves in Jewish history with the green-screen effect, showcase Jewish customs, reveal behind-the-scenes takes on the matchmaking "industry," and even go "live" to broadcast antisemitic attacks in Israel and the United States in real time.

Combating (Human) Hate on TikTok

"TikTok has a Nazi problem." This red flag was being waved back at the beginning of 2019 when *Motherboard* published one of the first comprehensive examinations of the dark side of TikTok under this title.[1] The article traces examples of "blatant, violent white supremacy and Nazism" in profiles that support and encourage the murder of Jews and Black people. Accompanied by antisemitic caricatures of Jewish figures and Nazi symbols, anonymous neo-Nazi users were posting "all jews must die" and "kill the fucking Jews." In response, some Jewish TikTok accounts reused the videos to direct the platform's attention to this stream of hate. TikTok's moderation system was still in its early stages due to the app only having been available in the US market since 2018, but the company promised better regulation and addressed the situation as "a challenge for the industry as a whole."[2]

Since then, TikTok has become the subject of many regulatory concerns, leading countries like Indonesia and India to ban the application, as well as class-action lawsuits in the United States over national security issues, child privacy, pro-violence content, and more.[3] The number of hate videos on TikTok has skyrocketed in the past two years, resulting in a "seismic increase" of 912% in antisemitic tropes, images, rhetoric, and comments in 2021.[4] Similar to trends on YouTube, Facebook, Twitter, and Instagram, the distribution of antisemitic content on social media increased across languages,[5] and strategies like appropriating hashtags (e.g., #Auschwitz, #Jews) has led content to be "highly offensive and discriminatory in nature."[6] TikTok's immense popularity, together with an algorithmic infrastructure that often lends prominence to controversial content, has opened the gate for those who seek to use the platform "to promote, support or encourage hatred and extremism."[7]

In 2020, a report from *The Sun* revealed that the app exposes teens to a "cesspit of hate" while praising terrorists and encouraging Holocaust denial.[8] The investigation revealed a series of highly engaging videos featuring antisemitic symbols such as caricatures of Jewish men with large noses or the existence of profiles like @Holo-hoax or @CovidCaust cynically disparaging the Holocaust. For example, users co-opted a popular "duet" featuring a TikToker talking about the dangers of antisemitic slurs, combining it with another video showing a user opening an oven door and pointing inside as a reference to the cremation of Jews in the Holocaust. The wild circulation of harmful content led TikTok to score a "C" on the Simon Wiesenthal Center's digital terrorism and hate report card for how social media platforms combat extremism.[9]

Compared to other platforms, TikTokers spread hate especially quickly because the infrastructure encourages trending audiovisual memes or videos that are "geared toward imitation and replication."[10] TikTok trends relying mainly on sounds and images serve as a "driving template and organizing principle for content."[11] This makes the experience for content creators more immediate, intuitive, and autodidactic, leading to the memeification of antisemitism on TikTok, such as in the case of "If I Were a Rich Man," from the Jewish cultural touchstone *Fiddler on the Roof.* This song became an audiovisual trend and a popular Expressify filter in which TikTokers filmed themselves singing with exaggerated facial expressions. Soon enough, antisemitic spreaders co-opted this trend and repackaged it as a template for hate by using it to resemble the "happy merchant," an antisemitic meme praised by the alt-right and identified as a hate symbol by the Anti-Defamation League.[12]

"Our cultural symbols are being hijacked on TikTok," mentioned one of the JewToks during our interviews. "Haters can take any video that I upload that has to do with Judaism and give it an antisemitic remix." Similar to the reactions to the *Fiddler* sound, JewToks try to reclaim visibility on the platform by encouraging their online communities to interact with their videos, keeping their original trends circulating on the For You page (FYP) or the audio-track main page. "This is a war on our Jewish existence in TikTok," added one of the JewToks.[13]

Contextualized in TikTok's participatory culture, this memetic "war" between users over Jewish narratives exposes a communalized force that undermines TikTok's familiar logic. Though considered an individualistic, content-driven platform in which interpersonal connectivity is downplayed, JewToks testify to a profound social collaboration when, for example, a "JewTok-friend is being raided by trolls." Moreover, the platform's vernacular supports new modes of sociality[14] that enable the creation of protected spaces for empathetically communicating Jewish sentiment, "especially when such spaces may not be physically available or where safety is a concern."[15]

Combating (Algorithmic) Hate on TikTok

JewToks' practice of fighting against hate speech serves as a double-edged sword. On the one hand, the utilization of the platform's unique quality of templatability enables JewToks to successfully fight hate creators and have "one united 'voice' to which they can creatively add their personal storyline"[16] while raising awareness of antisemitism. On the other hand, TikTok's algorithm poses a threat to their ability to use the platform to fight antisemitism because TikTok's moderation system tends to block and identify JewToks as spreaders of violent content due to their memetic use (e.g., altering, repacking, or remixing) of antisemitic content.

This internal contradiction in TikTok's algorithmic moderation came up in one of our interviews:

> When I encounter antisemitism content on TikTok, I know I'll face even a more frustrating challenge than combating the troll, and that is TikTok's algorithm. According to protocol, I need to alert TikTok on the troll's activity, but the report systems take days and even weeks to react. So, to effectively fight antisemitism, I need to creatively reuse the troll's existing hate content, whether by its comments or its own generated content…but most of the time, JewToks who counter speech are the ones to be flagged and shut off for days by the algorithm due to 'violation of terms'…in the meantime, trolls can spread hate freely.

JewToks consider TikTok's algorithm to be a black box in which "complexity and technical opacity hid[e] and obfuscate[e] their inner workings."[17] When it comes to the mysterious "algorithm regime"[18] of YouTube, Facebook, or Twitter, researchers have unpacked various aspects, revealing controversial algorithmic moderation ranging from user's performance of sexual identity[19] to the tendency for infrastructural racism,[20] and users' resistance to algorithmic power and oppression.[21] Meanwhile, in response to growing pressure from numerous stakeholders, TikTok has revealed aspects of the algorithmic logic powering its recommendation system,[22] in which users' interests and preferences are analyzed through their interactions with content to construct a personalized and curated FYP.[23]

Some scholars have attempted to unpack the operations and implications of TikTok's recommendation and moderation algorithms. For example, the algorithm's potential for enhancements of sociopolitical identity has been researched in the context of President Trump and the #TulsaFlop,[24] or user's beliefs about the TikTok algorithm[25] and its role in the distribution and representation of LGBTQ+ content.[26] Some have even criticized TikTok's algorithmic ability to control users' visibility as an "authoritarian technology"[27] practice. Still, TikTok's "secret sauce" of how users take full agency of their visibility requires further inquiry, especially concerning its role in content moderation.

Conceptually, the instability of the platform's moderation system might be explained through TikTok's embrace of *imperfections*, unlike most other social media platforms. TikTok users are encouraged to create (and consume) content that contains aesthetic *flaws* without adhering to the organized schemes of other visual online cultures.[28] This imperfect visual grammar, featuring authentic, non-polished, affective, and messy content, generates a viral "creative chaos"[29] from which the algorithm is being "fed." Within this chaotic environment, the powerful yet inherently unstable algorithm tends to deliver imperfect, unorganized, and mostly unexpected moderation choices, like those we detail below. This correlation between the platform's chaotic and messy collection of content and its recurring algorithmic glitches might be seen as "a feature, not a bug of the online world."[30]

Whether it is infrastructurally intended or not, members of JewTok do not need "proof" to feel validation that they battle with TikTok's algorithm daily, and even full transparency on how the platform polices content will not automatically empower creators to gain visibility. In this sense, JewToks is not alone in the experience of algorithmic discrimination. For instance, in June 2020, during Black Lives Matter protests across the United States, Black activists accused TikTok of censoring popular #BLM posts and lowering their views.[31] TikTok admitted having a "technical glitch" and blamed the hate speech detector for being "triggered by this combination of words."[32] Similar complaints were made by TikTok's Black influencers about being flagged on TikTok's Marketplace for inappropriate content,[33] and by participants in the #BlackTikTokStrike who refused to choreograph original dances to a hit song due to misattribution and "hijacked" routines on the FYP by white imitators.[34] At the same time, TikTok has been accused of censoring support videos of pro-democracy protests in Hong Kong, which led to American concerns about TikTok's Chinese ownership.[35]

Although they require further improvements, TikTok's human and algorithmic moderation systems are intended to fight the penetration of hate speech, prejudices, and discrimination into the digital realm. In the meantime, JewToks raise concerns about the ability of TikTok's algorithms to potentially reinforce social, political, or cultural stereotypes outside of digitally mediated contexts.[36] One member of JewTok stated,

> Sadly, TikTok is the perfect place for educating or even encouraging trolls to hurt Jews on the streets. I will not be shocked to find out that a future assassin was 'raised' in and by TikTok. The algorithm 'teaches' him that he can spread hate and get away with it.

JewToks believe that prevention must start by humanizing the Jewish community. With this in mind, we now turn our attention to selected videos from JewTok's members and analyze how they educate on Judaism as part of their creative combat against antisemitism on TikTok.

JewToks Fight Antisemitism: Dance, Humor, and Creativity

Prominent JewToks mainly perform two strategies to respond to antisemitic distortion and hate. The first strategy contributes to a different image of Jews and Judaism on TikTok and utilizes the platform to educate about Jewish history, culture, and religious customs. This strategy points toward two interconnected directions: First, it offers a way to build a Jewish community on TikTok as a "safe space" that benefits from the algorithmic structure of the FYP which promotes content that closely adjusts to the users' interests. Second, it uses TikTok to react to questions or popular stereotypes related to Jews and Judaism. Thereby, JewTok accounts such as @thatjinjyjew (Moses & Zippora) or @thatrelatablejew (Sarah Haskell) create a more differentiated and complex image of Jews and Judaism on TikTok. "For decades, Jews have been trying to fight so many twisted ideas about Judaism. It is mainly because people are not exposed enough to our everyday. TikTok changed it. I am able to deal with stereotypes by using humor and dance. This really changes perceptions," said one of our interviewees.

The second strategy of JewToks is to mock antisemitic ideas and directly address antisemitic content on and through TikTok. The American JewTok duo Jewcrazy, for instance, playfully addresses anti-Jewish stereotypes such as Jews as being rich and having devil horns. They create relatable comedic content with a "Jewish twist" by using popular styles of expression on TikTok like over-exaggeration and irony. This strategy, common among other JewTok profiles, reveals antisemitic resentments as such and simultaneously points toward the irrational and inconsistent character of enduring antisemitic imagery. "Everyone knows that those vicious narratives are old as time but still holds on to that. In this context, TikTok functions as a tool for not only combating toxic beliefs but also welcomes ignorant users that suddenly see how stupid it is to believe that Jews are monsters or malicious people," added another JewTok interviewee.

Both strategies enhance the visibility of American JewToks and integrate Jewish perspectives into the algorithmically organized social media environment of the platform. These videos utilize the dialogic structure of the app by responding to both Jewish and non-Jewish TikTokers. Moses & Zippora, an American Jewish Orthodox couple, refer to questions posted by users in their explanatory videos about Orthodox Jewish customs and traditions. Jewcrazy reacts to antisemitic comments, sometimes addressing specific comments directly. JewToks adjust their Jewish perspectives and content to the variety of trends provided by the platform. For example, Sarah Haskell, who empowers her Jewish identity by communicating Jewish sisterhood, creatively builds on the memetic nature of the platform. Haskell created a "Shabbat-transformation-meme" utilizing techniques usually used for fashion, time travel, or character transformations. In her memes, Haskell celebrates the beginning of the Shabbat—in itself a transformative moment in each week of the Jewish calendar—by filming herself in casual clothes, doing a sudden movement as a transition, and then appearing in a festive Shabbat dress. Haskell's Shabbat meme interconnects modern Jewish life with typical TikTok vernaculars: performance, dance, fashion, and transformation.

In their Rosh Hashana video celebrating the Jewish New Year, Moses & Zippora perform a similar move to Haskell. Seated in their kitchen and dressed casually, they stand up from their chairs and move toward the camera when they suddenly change and transform into festively dressed, Orthodox Jews bearing the typical signs of the holiday—a Shofar, honey, and an apple. In so doing, they emphasize the special character of the high holidays in the Jewish life circle and the transformative moment indicated by this shift. They also reconnect the appearance of religious Jews as a strange and different other to ordinary and everyday spaces and life situations shared with non-Jewish TikTokers.

Many JewToks include one of the best-known characteristics of the platform: dance. All JewToks discussed in this chapter utilize dancing for building "explanatory choreographies" while connecting with the platform and its particular aesthetics. In some of their videos, Zippora uses dance to combat old beliefs that Orthodox Jewish women are prohibited to dance in front of men while dancing with Moses. The duo Jewcrazy introduces an ironic tone while dancing as an act of resistance to stereotypical comments that attempt to mock the dance culture associated with the Jewish religion, such as "Jews got no rhythm." As a reaction, they suddenly jump on the kitchen countertop and perform a synchronized, dazzling, and ecstatically fast dance. @oochdawg (Michael), another leading member of JewTok, utilizes TikTok's culture of co-opting challenges and performing in the foreground of other TikTokers' memes to raise awareness of antisemitic ideas.

The case of Sarah Haskell highlights the declaratory function of the JewTok fight. In an exemplary video, she asserts that she will not stop acting as a proud Jew even though she is confronted with antisemitic comments. Haskell's videos adopt typical elements from the TikTok environment such as dance moves and lip-syncs or the superimposition of short texts. In doing so, Haskell presents herself as immersed in TikTok logic, demonstrating that TikTok *is* her natural environment and that she communicates with the authority of a TikTok creator. At the same time, she connects this 'safe space' to her own Jewish identity. Her speaking position as a TikToker merges with her speaking position as an American Jew. Thereby, TikTok becomes a "Jewish" space, and whoever attacks her as a Jewish creator is marked as an intruder of this space. Though Haskell does not directly attack any concrete expressions of hate speech, her TikTok labels such attacks as alien to the communication platform that she appropriates for Jewish expressions.

The Jewish TikTok creator Michael uses different tools to counter hate speech and antisemitism. He adopts the narrative structure of an edited self-conversation, presenting himself as a Jewish TikToker and as a TikTok user asking his alter ego about his experiences. These videos show what "love" looks like in the comments section on TikTok. Further, utilizing the green screen effect, these TikToks address viewers through a didactically arranged short narrative film that ends with screenshots from antisemitic comments as the punch line. Reusing TikTok material and merging it with newly generated content is another popular form of appropriation on the platform, which here is utilized for the purpose of problematizing and countering hate speech without offering space for harassing TikTokers.

In the case of Jewcrazy, they mainly mock anti-Jewish stereotypes in their TikToks. They utilize the theatrical dimension of the app to create playful videos that contain short ironic or comic miniatures. Responding to the popular #QuestionsIGetAsked challenge, they posted the version "Questions we get asked as Jews," which addressed topics such as the use of electricity on Shabbat, the antisemitic stereotype that Jews own banks, and the myth that Jews own space lasers. By overplaying stereotypes ("Jews are rich"), they respond to antisemitic discourses on TikTok in a playful way while harnessing the platform's ludic vernacular. At the same time, they also mock Jewish traditions such as the Brit Milah, the circumcision of Jewish boys after their eighth day, in many of their TikToks. In "Dance moves for Jews at a party," they shift from the classic "Travolta Dance" in Quentin Tarantino's *Pulp Fiction* (1994) to a gesture imitating scissors.

Jewish TikTokers also reference other JewToks and antisemitic attacks on fellow Jewish TikTokers with the help of the duet function. For example, Haskell expressed her solidarity with a fellow Jewish TikToker who was censored for "hate speech" after being reported by anti-Jewish trolls in a duet with Melinda Strauss. Jewcrazy performed a duet with Michael which utilized a dance trend to address antisemitic resentments. In doing so, Jewcrazy expressed their support for his attempt to challenge antisemitic posts ("When they get 6 million of you, yet you still manage to 'run the world'"). Utilizing trending dance elements as well as additional ironic textual layers ("On our way to the secret bank owners meeting"), these TikToks represent complex and multilayered attempts to establish Jewish spaces on the platform and react to anti-Jewish and antisemitic expressions.

Conclusion

One of our JewTok interviewees summed up the community's motivations with particular eloquence, saying, "As Jews on TikTok, our fight for our community's legitimacy is never-ending. It can be human hate trolls or the algorithm itself—the threat keeps on changing when it comes to TikTok. However, we need to make an impact in the real world. This needs to be our goal. This is why we are so motivated to make lemonade out of TikTok's lemons when it comes to fighting and educating people about their misunderstandings and blind hate against Jews. We have creative, engaging, and highly visible tools for that on TikTok, and although we are struggling, we believe TikTok is the place to start this change."

While hate speech, racism, and antisemitism are a disturbing, sad, and toxic reality on TikTok (as on other social media platforms), the app also facilitates subversive counter strategies and the establishment of particularly "Jewish" creative spaces and communities. JewToks have developed different strategies to counter antisemitism and hate speech. Some present a different image of Jews and

Judaism that contradicts dominant stereotypes and simultaneously educates about Jewish traditions and customs. Others directly confront antisemitism and hate speech by responding to other TikTokers or screenshots of antisemitic comments. At the same time, they utilize the playful environment provided by the app to establish a creative Jewish space. Connecting with other Jewish creators and intersecting TikTok aesthetics with Jewish traditions and customs, Jewish American life, and culture become an integral part of the diverse environment provided by and constituted through TikTok and its creators.

Notes

1 Joseph Cox, "TikTok Has a Nazi Problem," *Motherboard*, December 18, 2018, accessed September 9, 2021, https://www.vice.com/en/article/yw74gy/tiktok-neo-nazis-white-supremacy.
2 Ibid.
3 Justin Sherman, "Unpacking TikTok, Mobile Apps and National Security Risks," *Lawfare*, April 2, 2020, accessed July 16, 2020, https://www.lawfareblog.com/unpacking-tiktok-mobile-apps-and-national-security-risks.
4 Jordan Pike, "Antisemitic Content on TikTok Increases by 912%—Study," *The Jerusalem Post*, July 12, 2021, accessed September 25, 2020, https://www.jpost.com/diaspora/antisemitism/antisemitic-content-on-tiktok-increases-by-912-percent-study-673588.
5 Ahmed Omar, Tarek M Mahmoud and Tarek Abd-El-Hafeez, "Comparative Performance of Machine Learning and Deep Learning Algorithms for Arabic Hate Speech Detection in OSNS." In *The International Conference on Artificial Intelligence and Computer Vision*. Springer, Cham, April 2020: 247–257.
6 Gemma Commane and Rebekah Potton. "Instagram and Auschwitz: A Critical Assessment of the Impact Social Media Has on Holocaust Representation," *Holocaust Studies*, 25, nos. 1–2 (2019): 172.
7 Ciaran O'Connor, "Hatescape: An In-Depth Analysis of Extremism and Hate Speech on TikTok," *Institute for Strategic Dialogue*, 24 Aug. 2021, https://www.isdglobal.org/isd-publications/hatescape-an-in-depth-analysis-of-extremism-an d-hate-speech-on-tiktok/, 2021: 7.
8 Richard Wheatstone and Ciaran O'Connor, "TikTok Swamped with Sickening Videos of Terror Attacks Murders, Holocaust Denials and Vile Racist Slurs," *The Sun Online*, March 1, 2020, accessed May 15, 2020, https://www.thesun.co.uk/news/10962862/tiktok-extremist-racist-videos-anti-semitism/.
9 Simon Wiesenthal Center, "Digital Hate on Social Media," 2021, accessed September 29, 2021, https://www.wiesenthal.com/assets/pdf/holocaust-denial-on-social.pdf.
10 Diana Zulli and David James Zulli, "Extending the Internet Meme: Conceptualizing Technological Mimesis and Imitation Publics on the TikTok Platform," *New Media & Society* (2021): 10, https://doi.org/10.1177/1461444820983603.

11 Jing Zeng and Crystal Abidin, "OkBoomer, Time to Meet the Zoomers': Studying the Memefication of Intergenerational Politics on TikTok," *Information, Communication and Society* (2021): 24(16), 2459–2481.

12 Joel Finkelstein, Savvas Zannettou, Barry Bradlyn, and Jeremy Blackburn, "A Quantitative Approach to Understanding Online Antisemitism," 2018, *arXiv preprint arXiv:1809.01644.*

13 For a profound understanding of the Jewish community on TikTok, we conducted six in-depth interviews with creators who identify themselves as "JewToks." As most of the Jewish creators blocked the option to approach them directly via TikTok's direct messages, we traced 11 popular Jewish TikTokers (as stated in their profile activity) by scrolling on TikTok and contacted them via Instagram's DM. Six consented to our requests and were promised with anonymity for the purpose of sharing their reflections without fear or any judgment.

14 danah boyd, "Social Networks as Networked Publics: Affordances, Dynamics, and Implications," in *A Networked Self: Identity, Community, and Culture on Social Network Sites*, ed. Zizi Paparcharissi (New York: Routledge, 2011), 39–58.

15 Ellen Simpson and Bryan Semaan, "For You, or for "You"? Everyday LGBTQ+ Encounters with TikTok," *Proceedings of the ACM on Human-Computer Interaction* 4 (2021): 252.

16 Zeng and Abidin, "OkBoomer, Time to Meet the Zoomers': Studying the Memefication of Intergenerational Politics on TikTok," 12.

17 Nicholas Diakopoulos, "Algorithmic Accountability," *Digital Journalism* 3, no. 3 (2015): 404.

18 Michael A. DeVito, Darren Gergle, and Jeremy Birnholtz, "'Algorithms Ruin Everything:' #RIPTwitter, Folk Theories, and Resistance to Algorithmic Change in Social Media," *Proceedings of the 2017 CHI Conference on Human Factors in Computing Systems*, May 2017: 3163–3174.

19 Tobias Raun, *Out Online: Trans Self-Representation and Community Building on YouTube*, (London and New York: Routledge, 2016).

20 Ariadna Matamoros-Fernández, "Platformed Racism: The Mediation and Circulation of an Australian Race-Based Controversy on Twitter, Facebook and YouTube," *Information, Communication & Society* 20, no. 6 (2017): 930–946.

21 Emiliano Treré, "From Digital Activism to Algorithmic Resistance," in *The Routledge Companion to Media and Activism*, ed. Graham Meikle (London: Routledge, 2018): 367–375.

22 Louise Matsakis, "How TikTok's 'For You' Algorithm Works," *Wired*, June 18, 2020, accessed October 1, 2021, https: //www.wired.com/story/ tiktok-finally-explains-for-you-algorithm-works/.

23 Benjamin Guinaudeau, Fabio Vottax, and Kevin Munger, "Fifteen Seconds of Fame: TikTok and the Democratization of Mobile Video on Social Media," working paper, 2020, accessed October 1, 2021, https://osf.io/f7ehq/.

24 Jack Bandy and Nicholas Diakopoulos, "#TulsaFlop: A Case Study of Algorithmically-Influenced Collective Action on TikTok," *arXiv preprint arXiv:2012.07716*, 2020: 1–7.

25 Daniel Klug, Yiluo Qin, Morgan Evans, and Geoff Kaufman, "Trick and Please. A Mixed-Method Study on User Assumptions about the TikTok Algorithm." *13th ACM Web Science Conference 2021*, June 2021: 84–92.

26 Ellen Simpson and Bryan Semaan, "For You, or for 'You'? Everyday LGBTQ+ Encounters with TikTok," *Proceedings of the ACM on Human-Computer Interaction* 4, CSCW3 (2021): 1–34.
27 Bandy and Diakopoulos, "#TulsaFlop," 1–7.
28 E. Bresnick, "Intensified Play: Cinematic Study of TikTok Mobile App," *Research Gate*, 2019, accessed January 5, 2020, www.researchgate. net/publication/335570557_Intensified_Play_ Cinematic_study_of_ TikTok_mobile_app.
29 Katie Elson Anderson, "Getting Acquainted with Social Networks and Apps: It Is Time to Talk about TikTok," *Library Hi Tech News* (2020): 37(4), pp. 7–12
30 Ibid.
31 Sam Shead, "TikTok Apologizes after Being Accused of Censoring #BlackLivesMatter Posts," *CNBC*, June 2, 2020, accessed October 1, 2021, https:// www.cnbc.com/2020/06/02/tiktok-blacklivesmatter-censorship.html.
32 Todd Spangler, "TikTok Blames 'Technical Glitch' for Suppressing View Counts on #BlackLivesMatter, #GeorgeFloyd Videos," *Variety*, June 2, 2020, accessed October 1, 2021, https://variety.com/2020/digital/news/tiktok-suppressed-view-counts-blacklivesmatter-georgefloyd-videos-1234622975/.
33 Shirin Gaffary, "How TikTok's Hate Speech Detection Tool Set off a Debate about Racial Bias on the App," *Vox*, July 7, 2021, accessed October 1, 2021, https://www.vox.com/recode/2021/7/7/22566017/tiktok-black-creators-ziggi-tyler-debate-about-black-lives-matter-racial-bias-social-media.
34 Beatrice Forman, "Digital Blackface Led to TikTok's First Strike," *Vox*, June 29, 2021, accessed October 1, 2021, https://www.vox.com/the-goods/2021/6/29/22554596/digital-blackface-megan-thee-stallion-song-tiktok-first-strike.
35 Janko Roettgers, "Senators Call for TikTok Security Review over China Espionage Fears," *Variety*, October 24, 2019, accessed October 1, 2021, https://variety.com/2019/digital/news/tiktok-china-government-espionage-censorship-1203382097/.
36 Matthew Kay, Cynthia Matuszek, and Sean A. Munson, "Unequal Representation and Gender Stereotypes in Image Search Results for Occupations," *Proceedings of the 33rd Annual ACM Conference on Human Factors in Computing Systems* (2015), (CHI '15). (New York: Association for Computing Machinery), pp. 3819–3828.

Section Two

Gender and Sexuality on TikTok

5 Watching TikTok, Feeling Feminism

Intergenerational Flows of Feminist Knowledge

Shauna Pomerantz and Miriam Field

On March 3, 2021, Sarah Everard, a 33-year-old marketing executive, went missing while walking home in South London. On March 10, her dismembered body was found in the woods near Kent. Wayne Couzens, a constable with the Metropolitan Police Service, subsequently pled guilty to Everard's kidnapping, rape, and murder. The high-profile case ignited outrage in the United Kingdom and across the global north over violence against women, including the lack of prosecutions for sexual assaults.[1] Intensifying the anger, four women were arrested by MET officers at a peaceful vigil held for Everard on March 13 and dozens were detained for gathering unlawfully during COVID-19. A viral image of attendee Patsy Stevenson pinned down by police became emblematic of the lack of institutional support women receive in relation to their bodily safety.

Coverage of the crime and subsequent police aggression flooded the For You Page (FYP) of Miriam (age 12) and entered our breakfast conversation in Canada the morning after the vigil. She asked her mom, Shauna (age 50), "Did you hear about Sarah Everard's murder? I saw it on TikTok." Suddenly angry, she continued, "How can this happen? I'm afraid to go out alone. So many girls are hurt and sexually assaulted in their lives. It's not fair." Having seen the viral image of Stevenson circulate on TikTok, Miriam also wondered, "Why did the police do that? The women weren't hurting anyone. Why don't they arrest the men who hurt women?" "Show me the videos," Shauna responded, "and we can talk about it." As feminist writer and activist Sara Ahmed explains in her examination of how one comes to feminism, once you know that women are vulnerable, you feel changes in your body, "which [is] a different way of encountering the world." Ahmed notes that each experience of violence, each reminder that girls and women are not safe, enacts a cumulative affect: "You begin to feel a pressure, this relentless assault on the senses...The world is experienced as sensory intrusion. It is too much."[2]

DOI: 10.4324/9781003280705-8

While TikTok regularly entered our breakfast conversations, this was different. The sensory intrusion that Ahmed describes was on display as Miriam's head hung low. And Shauna, attuned to the weight of the issue, felt heavy. She remembered moments from her own childhood when she became aware of her vulnerability and how this made her body feel. Mindful that such fear can negatively impact a girl's life, Shauna neither wanted her daughter to be perpetually scared nor lack knowledge about how girls and women experience violence in the world. While needing to commiserate, Shauna also wanted to engage feminism as a logical response to the sensations Miriam was experiencing. Ahmed explains that,

> ...feminism is a sensible reaction to the injustices of the world, which we might register at first through our own experiences. We might work over, mull over, these experiences; we might keep coming back to them because they do not make sense. In other words we have to make sense of what does not make sense.[3]

When Miriam showed Shauna TikToks about Everard's murder at the breakfast table, and others during discussions to follow, we tried to make sense of what does not make sense, "of coming to register something that is difficult."[4] TikTok not only opened space for these conversations but participated in them as an accessible platform that concretized girls' and women's pain, anger, and protest in 15- to 60-second videos. As a powerful presence in our home, TikTok had always sparked conversation.[5] Its unique combination of video, sound, text, and performance brought Miriam closer to users' raw emotions about violence against women than Instagram ever could. As a result, TikTok catalyzed and took part in the flow of feminist knowledge between us, offering both an opportunity and a comfortable medium for important discussion.

Our chapter highlights TikTok as a facilitator of feminism and feminist dialogue among parents and children, including intersections of sexism and racism that make some stories more visible than others. When we watched TikToks, we became, and came to be part of, a feminist community. As we immersed ourselves in TikTok to learn about violence against women, we felt sadness and rage, but we were also put in touch with the power of collective political action. Feminist writer and activist bell hooks defines feminism as "a movement to end sexism, sexist exploitation, and oppression."[6] We only come to feminism, hooks explains, when we "understand sexism."[7] TikTok not only helped Miriam understand sexism and the possibilities inherent in feminism by offering her hundreds of girls' and women's experiences, but it also helped Shauna understand what Miriam knew about these issues and how she might contribute to furthering her feminist knowledge. TikTok also enabled us to feel feminism together when we assembled to make sense of incomprehensible things. As media scholar Melanie Kennedy explains, the most well-known voices on TikTok are teenage girls, confirming that they "rule the Internet right now."[8] TikTok was thus a familiar space that generated empathy and channeled Miriam's anger. In what follows, we explore this transmission of information through what we call "radical media engagement" as we watched and talked about TikToks connected to violence against women.[9]

Radical Media Engagement: Challenging "Official" Knowledge

TikTok is ubiquitous among Generation Z, or people born between the mid-1990s and early 2010s.[10] Initially known as the app for fun performances, TikTok has become "*the* platform for political activism" due to a clever algorithm that quickly spreads interconnected information.[11] While TikTok was once heavily criticized for censoring content that did not "fit its carefully crafted carefree image,"[12] hundreds of anti-oppression hashtags now proliferate on the app. As a result, "77% of TikTok users say that TikTok has helped them learn about social justice and politics,"[13] through hashtags, such as #BlackLivesMatter, #GunViolence, #Feminism, #GirlPower, and #BeTheChange. While concerns over "inappropriate" content, safety issues, and data mining are ongoing,[14] it is clear that TikTok exposes young people to social justice movements sooner than if they were not on the app, causing pundits to claim that "TikTok teens will save the world."[15]

Though TikTok has increased young people's political awareness, some parents' lack of knowledge about the app often precludes them from valuing its potential.[16] Miriam explained that parents may understand the information "but not the TikTok, like, how it's made and the style we're getting the information in. It's a different way of communicating than what you would see on the news." To remedy this digital divide, Miriam offered some advice:

> I think what [kids] need to do is just sit down with their parents and...just show them how it works and show them what videos they're making and, like, explain to them and let them ask you questions and just answer them honestly.

This intergenerational, multidirectional approach comprises our autoethnographic method of radical media engagement. While autoethnography is a qualitative technique that connects the "autobiographical and personal to the cultural, social, and political,"[17] radical media engagement specifically focuses on how a media form, such as TikTok, is part of a broader, interconnected network that mediates parent-child relations.[18] Rather than a unidirectional form of instruction, radical media engagement is "multidirectional and contributes to the diverse assemblages in which parents and children are embedded,"[19] thus highlighting a media form as not just coextensive with children's lives, but parents' lives as well. With this acknowledgment, the goal of radical media engagement is to open flows of knowledge transmission, making children the experts who help their parents understand what they do online. This method creates opportunities for children to engage their parents in a way that destabilizes traditional power structures predicated on a hierarchy where adults always know more and better, and children are always limited by innocence and inexperience.

A growing body of literature explores the importance of social media for girls' participation in and cultivation of feminist politics.[20] This literature argues that online feminism in the form of blogs, memes, social media posts, and their comments comprise powerful forms of knowledge transmission that help "develop [girls'] burgeoning feminist identities."[21] Digital media scholars Crystal Kim and Jessica Ringrose suggest that we pay greater attention to online feminist participation to challenge what counts as "official" knowledge, noting that social media is cast outside of school-sanctioned curricula even though it is where young people spend time, learn about current events, and communicate with each other. Adding to the discussion of how social media offer "girls important tools for civic engagement,"[22] we focus on feminist knowledge transmission between parents and children. For this chapter, we draw on two unstructured, digitally recorded conversations where we watched and talked about TikToks relating to Everard's murder. Our method participates in transforming the digital divide that separates parents and children by encouraging robust, non-judgmental conversations about media that matter to young people. In so doing, radical media engagement challenges the adult authority that perpetuates hierarchical relations between parents and children through the devaluation of youth digital spaces, such as TikTok.

#97percent, #NotAllMen, and #BWLM: Living a Feminist Life on TikTok

Miriam and Shauna watched TikToks labeled with two hashtags that proliferated on the app after Everard's murder: #97percent and #NotAllMen. The former was based on a study in the United Kingdom that stated 97% of women ages 18–24, and 70% of all women, have experienced sexual harassment.[23] In response, #NotAllMen circulated to deflect responsibility for these staggering statistics. Miriam showed Shauna several videos protesting #NotAllMen, including a TikTok by @perfectly_patience2.0, in which a young woman sings: "Not all men, but you'd still look under her skirt if you had a chance. Not all men, but she still walks to her car with keys between her fingers." After watching, Miriam explained her feelings about the hashtag:

> Like, people who use #NotAllMen are trying to make it about *them* when it's not. Like, there was a guy who posted a TikTok that said, 'Yeah, we get it, girls get raped, but so do guys!' right after Sarah's murder. So, I commented, 'Yeah guys totally do get raped, but right now we're trying to focus on girls and what happened and you posting this is just showing that you're not supporting us.'

To further her point, Miriam wanted Shauna to see the difference between what girls and boys were posting after Everard's murder. @shaylarogers21 compiled screen grabs from multiple TikToks to highlight these differences with the caption: "Boys, your silence is getting really f*cking loud." Describing the video, Miriam noted that girls were posting information and support for women who had experienced violence, and boys were posting, "all these basketball, irrelevant things that are not what you need to be posting right now. So, the TikTok is about how some guys don't care and it shows." "What about boys you know?" Shauna asked. Even more frustrated, Miriam noted that, "They weren't posting anything to show they cared, and, like, boys I know are always making jokes online about rape. Like, 'I'll rape your mom' is a common thing. Or sometimes, they'll even be, like, 'She's so pretty, I'd rape her.' And we always fight back against them and say, 'That's not funny. No one's laughing.'"

While Miriam began using TikTok in 2017 to learn viral dances with her friends, she was also exposed to what caused her to "sense an injustice."[24] Everard's murder was not her initial introduction to violence against women, but it brought a tidal wave of TikToks to her FYP that detailed traumatic experiences, including disapproving comments about what girls and women were wearing when sexually assaulted, taunts of disbelief because victims could have "just pushed him off," and countless videos describing how someone became incorporated into the 97%. As part of "coming up against the world,"[25] Miriam also watched TikToks that helped her identify sexual harassment. A viral video responding to #NotAllMen by @patronsaintoflesbians asked viewers to fold one finger down if they had experienced any of the following: received unsolicited dick pics, been begged for nudes, been catcalled, been followed, been repeatedly asked out after saying "no," heard inappropriate comments or jokes about your body, or been leered at in public. The TikTok concludes with, "If you have even one finger down, you have been sexually harassed and I am so sorry." Shauna looked at Miriam's hand to see four fingers folded. When she expressed surprise, Miriam said: "That's why it's 97%. It's everywhere. Like, boys message me over socials, 'You send?' Or, like, 'How freaky are you?' and if you say you are, then they'll continue [to ask for nudes], but if you say, 'I'm not', they'll get the message." But rather than see their request as "wrong," getting the message simply meant that the boy moved on to someone else.[26]

Hearing these experiences caused Shauna to understand that her daughter had been dealing with more sexual harassment than she knew. "Yeah, but it's helped me realize some things," Miriam offered. "I stand for girls. I believe in girls' rights. I feel that girls should be treated equally to boys." Buoyed by this statement, Shauna replied: "I love that you're a feminist. I'm a feminist, too." Ahmed suggests that, "Feminism often begins with intensity: you are aroused by what you come up against. You register something in the sharpness of an impression."[27] It was clear that TikTok had facilitated Miriam's feminism by not only exposing her to the pain and anger of gender injustice, but also by providing a language for collective political action, as well as space for feminist community (see Mendes et al., 2019). "It sounds like you've learned a lot from TikTok," Shauna suggested. "Yeah," Miriam responded, "like, as a girl, TikTok has paved a path that I can follow, showing me things that I can take into my life and things I can do. There's *a lot* of girl power on TikTok!" "But," Shauna added, "it isn't a utopia for girls, is it? Like girls get harassed on TikTok, too." "It's both," Miriam replied. "But if there's a negative TikTok blaming girls for something then there'll be a bunch of comments that say, 'How embarrassing for you to say that' or 'How stupid.' Like, we fight back!"

Focusing on other types of inequality, Shauna asked Miriam if she knew why Sarah Everard had received so much attention. Miriam thought it was because the crime was committed by a police officer. Shauna agreed, but also offered another perspective: "It's because she was a pretty, young, white woman with a good job and a boyfriend." The intensive media coverage of Everard's murder drew attention to the relative absence of reporting on violence against Black and Indigenous women, women of color, non-binary people, and trans women.[28] Ahmed stresses that a movement to end sexism and sexual oppression, "cannot be separated from racism...Intersectionality is a starting point, the point from which we must proceed if we are to offer an account of how power works."[29] To focus on racism in relation to sexism, we first reflected on discussions from May 2020, when Miriam showed Shauna TikToks about George Floyd, an African American man murdered by white Minneapolis police officer Derek Chauvin.[30] We discussed how systemic racism meant that Floyd was treated differently by police because he was Black and how our whiteness operates as privilege.

Linking to sexism, Shauna then showed Miriam TikToks about Breonna Taylor, a Black woman from Louisville, Kentucky, who was shot dead by police while asleep on March 13, 2020. When no charges were laid for her murder, @thevictoriastory made a TikTok under the hashtag #BWLM (Black Women's Lives Matter) in which she said, "Today's decision felt like the last nail in the coffin for all the disrespect Black woman have been facing recently." After we watched, Shauna asked "Do you know why that hashtag exists?" Thinking for a moment, Miriam responded:

> ...because not only Black Lives Matter, you also have to think about Black women because they not only get racist things told to them, but they also get sexual things. Like, me, I get sexist things said to me but not racist things, but Black girls and women get both, they get double the amount of harassment.

"So, yeah," Shauna pursued, "you understand why a girl or woman who is Black or Indigenous is more oppressed in the world?" "Well," Miriam began slowly, "people seem to care a lot less about Black and Indigenous girls getting hurt. Like, it isn't hyped as much." Agreeing, Shauna added, "Sarah's story was big headlines, but Breonna's story was buried..." Interjecting, Miriam said, "Because people are racist." "Yeah," Shauna continued, "and because a white woman's life is seen as more valuable than a Black or Indigenous woman's life..." Interrupting again, Miriam stated emphatically: *"Even though it's not, actually."*

Radical media engagement made space for these and other important conversations to emerge. Because it is a method based on intergenerational, multidirectional flows of knowledge concentrated around a media form that is interconnected with parent-child relations it not only helped us hear each other, but it also authorized TikTok as a valid source for feminist knowledge outside of "official" formats. Reflecting on how social media circumvents adult-sanctioned school-based learning or the unidirectional transmission of information from parent to child, Shauna asked: "Do you think that's an interesting shift nowadays, that girls get their information from TikTok?" "Yeah," Miriam replied,

> ...because I feel like when you were a kid, you didn't have TikTok and your parents sometimes wouldn't tell you, or tell you enough, or even tell you the truth to hide it from you thinking it would keep you safe. But now, there's really no hiding anything. Like, you might have not told me about Sarah Everard, so I didn't worry or stress. But now, if I wanted to know anything, I would just watch a TikTok. I feel like I know *everything.*

Miriam's comments accentuate the power of TikTok as a source of information for young people. Challenging the hierarchical arrangement of adult authority versus childhood innocence, TikTok's popularity with Gen Z suggests that young people are not only hungry for this information but ready to receive it. As Miriam said when Shauna asked how much of her knowledge about violence against women comes from TikTok: "Like, *all of it.*"

Close to Home: TikTok as Feminist Theory

As an entrenched part of youth culture brimming with debates over sexism and feminism, TikTok offers a place for young people to learn about the experiences of others while also acquiring a language to describe things that have happened to them. Ahmed contends that "we generate feminist theory by living a feminist life."[31] For Miriam and countless others, TikTok comprises a form of feminist theory because it is where a feminist life may be born, cultivated, and protected vis-à-vis short videos and comments that inspire feminist practice both on- and offline. As Miriam explained when asked by Shauna why she is feminist: "I think it's the right thing to believe in and sometimes girls don't have a lot of power and feminism gives us a sense of power, that we can do something together to make it better." For Miriam, living a feminist life means living it on TikTok, where videos are political statements, likes are declarations, and comments are rebuttals linked to broader identity negotiations. These conversations travel seamlessly across on- and offline worlds, making TikTok relevant and important in real life as it informs daily actions and beliefs.

Ahmed suggests that if "we start close to home, we open ourselves out" and, in so doing, see "how our own struggles to make sense of realities that are difficult to grasp become part of a wider struggle..."[32]

For parents, TikTok offers an invitation to learn about and participate in how their child may be struggling to make sense of things through a familiar medium. TikTok offers parents the opportunity to connect with their child and learn about their experiences, viewpoints, fears, and triumphs. TikTok may give parents insight into how their child is living a feminist life, the sexism and racism they may be facing but have not talked about, and the moments of pride they may have felt when posting or commenting about something that made them want to take a stand. When Shauna watched the "put a finger down challenge" with Miriam and learned that she had encountered many kinds of sexual harassment, while difficult it also made her realize that her daughter was more aware and involved than she knew; it made her cognizant not just of her daughter's feminism, but of her *need* for feminism. And when Miriam heard Shauna talking about Breonna Taylor, she became aware that girls and women of color experience sexism differently through interlocking systems of oppression that intensify harassment. We learned from each other in flows that were not curtailed by adult authority, judgment, or panic. We learned from each other because we had knowledge to share with and understand from one another.

Our method of radical media engagement promotes multidirectional flows of knowledge between parents and children, not to silence parents or reverse familial power dynamics, but to challenge a hierarchy predicated on adult authority and childhood innocence that devalues children's knowledge. The goal is for parents to better understand what their children do online and to increase parents' awareness of knowledge transmission through digital platforms. The goal is also to engage in egalitarian conversations that do not default to negative verdicts predicated on lack of information. While many parents support their child's interests, often this support is dispensed from a distance. Through accessing the spaces where children are, radical media engagement shrinks digital divides and challenges "official" knowledge as the only kind that may benefit young people. This effort offers parents the opportunity to learn from their children, and children, sensing this interest, may be more open to learning from their parents.

Because feminism is often housed in "official" settings, hooks advocates for its transmission through non-academic sources: "We need work that is especially geared towards youth culture," reaching "beyond the academic and even the written world…Books on tape, songs, radio, and television are all ways to share feminist knowledge."[33] To this list, we add TikTok. Beyond adult-sanctioned pedagogies, TikTok generates feminism close to home—at home—where parents and children may be sitting at the breakfast table trying to make sense of what does not make sense, where Miriam says, "I watched this TikTok about Sarah Everard's murder," and where Shauna says, "Show me."

Notes

1 Elian Peltier, "London Police Officer Pleads Guilty to Murdering Sarah Everard," *The New York Times*, July 9, 2021, https://www.nytimes.com/2021/07/09/world/europe/sarah-everard-wayne-couzens-murder-guilty.html.
2 Sara Ahmed, *Living a Feminist Life* (Durham, NC: Duke University Press, 2017), 23.
3 Ibid., 21.
4 Ibid.
5 Shauna Pomerantz and Miriam Field, "A TikTok Assemblage: Girlhood, Radical Media Engagement, and Parent–Child Generativity," in *Visual and Cultural Identity Constructs of Global Youth and Young Adults: Situated, Embodied and Performed Ways of Being, Engaging and Belonging*, ed. F. Blaikie (New York: Routledge, 2001), 139–157.
6 bell hooks, *Feminism Is for Everybody: Passionate Politics* (London: Pluto Press, 2000), 1.
7 Ibid.
8 Melanie Kennedy, "'If the Rise of the TikTok Dance and E-Girl Aesthetic Has Taught us Anything, It's That Teenage Girls Rule the Internet Right Now': TikTok Celebrity, Girls and the Coronavirus Crisis," *European Journal of Cultural Studies* 23, no. 6 (2020): 1069–1076.
9 Pomerantz and Field, "A TikTok Assemblage," 140–141.
10 Trevor Boffone, *Renegades: Digital Dance Cultures from Dubsmash to TikTok* (Oxford: Oxford University Press, 2021).
11 Nuurrianti Jalli, "How TikTok Can be the New Platform for Political Activism: Lessons from Southeast Asia," *The Conversation*, 2021, https://theconversation.com/how-tiktok-can-be-the-new-platform-for-political-activism-lessons-from-southeast-asia-155556. See also Katherine Hosie, "More Than Just Tok: Gen Z's Activism on TikTok is Outperforming the Performative," *Reach3*, 2020, https://www.reach3insights.com/blog/tiktok-social-activism.
12 Shelley Banjo, "TikTok Embraces Political Content for Black Lives Matter," *Aljazeera*, June 17, 2020, https://www.aljazeera.com/economy/2020/6/17/tiktok-embraces-political-content-for-black-lives-matter.
13 Hosie, "More Than Just Tok."
14 Common Sense Media, "Parents' Ultimate Guide to TikTok," March 5, 2021, https://www.commonsensemedia.org/blog/parents-ultimate-guide-to-tiktok
15 John Herrman, "TikTok Is Shaping Politics. But How?" *The New York Times*, June 28, 2020, https://www.nytimes.com/2020/06/28/style/tiktok-teen-politics-gen-z.html.
16 Alex Hern, "'Adults Don't Get it': Why TikTok Is Facing Greater Scrutiny," *The Guardian*, July 4, 2019, https://www.theguardian.com/technology/2019/jul/05/why-tiktok-is-facing-greater-scrutiny-video-sharing-app-child-safety.

17 Carolyn Ellis, *The Ethnographic I: A Methodological Novel about Autoethnography*. (Lanham, MD: Rowman Altamira, 2004), xix.

18 While this chapter is specifically about parent–child relations, other forms of intergenerational dialogue are relevant, such as teacher–student. For a powerful example of what this kind of radical media engagement can look like in the classroom, see Boffone, *Renegades*.

19 Pomerantz and Field, "A TikTok Assemblage," 140.

20 For examples, see Sue Jackson, "Young Feminists, Feminism and Digital Media," *Feminism & Psychology* 28, no. 1 (2018): 32–49. Jessalynn Keller, *Girls' Feminist Blogging in a Postfeminist Age* (New York: Routledge, 2015). Jessalynn Keller, Kaitlynn Mendes, and Jessica Ringrose, "Speaking 'Unspeakable Things': Documenting Digital Feminist Responses to Rape Culture," *Journal of Gender Studies* 27, no. 1 (2018): 22–36. Crystal Kim and Jessica Ringrose, "Stumbling Upon Feminism": Teenage Girls' Forays into Digital and School-Based Feminisms," *Girlhood Studies* 11, no. 2 (2018): 46–62. Kaitlynn Mendes, Jessica Ringrose, and Jessalynn Keller, *Digital Feminist Activism: Girls and Women Fight Back against Rape Culture* (Oxford: Oxford University Press. 2019). Carrie A. Rentschler, "Rape Culture and the Feminist Politics of Social Media," *Girlhood Studies* 7, no. 1 (2014): 65–82. Hanna Retallack, Jessica Ringrose, and Emilie Lawrence, "'Fuck your Body Image': Teen Girls' Twitter and Instagram Feminism in and Around School," in *Learning Bodies: The Body in Youth and Childhood Studies*, ed. Julia Coffey, Shelley Budgeon, and Helen Cahill (Singapore: Springer, 2016), 85–103.

21 Kim and Ringrose, "Stumbling Upon Feminism" 47.

22 Ibid.

23 UN Women United Kingdom, "Public Spaces Need to Be Safe and Inclusive for All. Now," https://www.unwomenuk.org/safe-spaces-now.

24 Ahmed, *Living a Feminist Life*, 21.

25 Ibid., 19.

26 See Jessica Ringrose, Katilyn Regehr, and Sophie Whitehead, "'Wanna Trade?' Cisheteronormative Homosocial Masculinity and the Normalization of Abuse in Youth Digital Sexual Image Exchange," *Journal of Gender Studies* (2021): online first.

27 Ahmed, *Living a Feminist Life*, 4.

28 Kate Manne, "What Sarah Everard's Murder Illuminates—and Might Obscure," *The Atlantic*, March 17, 2021, https://www.theatlantic.com/ideas/archive/2021/03/what-sarah-everards-murder-illuminatesand-might-obscure/618302/.

29 Ahmed, *Living a Feminist Life*, 5.

30 See Pomerantz and Field, "A TikTok Assemblage."

31 Ahmed, *Living a Feminist Life*, 89.

32 Ibid., 19–20.

33 hooks, *Feminism Is for Everybody*, 23–24.

6 "Do you want to form an alliance with me?"

Glimpses of Utopia in the Works of Queer Women and Non-Binary Creators on TikTok

Claudia Skinner

"Do you want to form an alliance with me?" asks the voice of Dwight Schrute of TV's *The Office*. Posing the question via lip-synch is TikTok creator Alayna Joy as part of a humorous imagining of how queer community is created.[1] The invitation for solidarity that this audio depicts can be considered representative of a particular type of dynamic that exists on Queer TikTok. "Do you want to form an alliance with me?" is the question that queer TikTok users and creators are extending to one another through their innovations and interactions on the app, inviting each other into their journey of identity performance, self-exploration, and sexual education. In so doing, they are building space for community and connection, a process that has been of particular importance during the COVID-19 pandemic due to confinement in homes that may not be supportive of their identities and isolation from queer support groups.[2]

In order to analyze the nature and impact of these moves toward community, this chapter utilizes the lens of José Esteban Muñoz's concept of "queer utopia." More specifically, this chapter focuses on the queer utopia that is being pursued on TikTok by queer women and non-binary people whose sexualities do not center men. My intent in focusing on this demographic is to contribute to the effort to fill in the gap in queer studies that has resulted from scholarly attention being skewed toward gay men.[3] In so doing, I wish to bring to the fore the culture and community of those whose experience and desire lies outside of the heteropatriarchal idealized gender. I look at two case studies—one being the trend of queer women and non-binary people utilizing TikTok to discuss or theatrically recreate their turning away from heteronormativity during the pandemic; and the second being a creator-specific case study that looks at the work and experiences of Archie Bongiovanni.

DOI: 10.4324/9781003280705-9

Queer Space and Utopia

The opportunity to create, configure, repurpose, and reclaim space for queer livelihoods has been a salve and refuge for LGBTQ+ peoples. The dance floor, the bathroom stall, the college campus safe space, a Pride festival parade route, or an affordable housing apartment— these spaces have been and are essential for survival and flourishing. However, these spaces have also long been fraught with violence. Police raids on gay and lesbian bars were frequent from the mid to late twentieth century, along with harassment and attacks from homophobic locals.[4] Despite what the image of rainbow-painted police cars may suggest, state violence against queer communities has not abated in the present day, as demonstrated by incidents such as the 2020 NYPD police assault on Pride month protestors.[5]

Owing to the COVID-19 pandemic, an already compromised relationship with space has been made more difficult for queer people and their communities, particularly for working-class queer communities and queer communities of color who are pushed out of potential spaces of belonging due to a system of white supremacist capitalism. The conditions of the pandemic necessitate transfigurations of the existing, predominantly in-person, practices involved in creating and sustaining community, and the performance of identity. Without such in-person spaces, social media apps, which have previously mostly functioned as complementary albeit increasingly prominent sites for queer sociality, have become the necessary alternative. One such social media app is TikTok. TikTok has seen a marked increase in users since social distancing began in March 2020, with lockdown being a major factor behind the exponential rise in TikTok's use and visibility.[6]

With TikTok users can edit videos within the app, utilizing a number of image filters, visual effects, and sound clips. Once a video is published, these visual and auditory effects are noted onscreen as a hyperlink that if selected by a viewer will offer them the opportunity to make their own video with that effect, enabling them to create their own riff on the narrative structure created by those effects. Their video will then be automatically entered into a catalog of videos that all use that particular effect. This reproducible but adaptable structure operates as a sort of palimpsest that allows for the development of community culture.

Diana Zulli and David James Zulli (2020) conclude that TikTok's infrastructure positions mimesis as the basis of sociality on the site, encouraging a novel type of networked public.[7] What is unique about the publics formed via TikTok, Zulli and Zulli argue, is that TikTok publics are not based on experiences that are interpersonal, discursive, or affective, but that they are largely processual.[8] Nonetheless, research demonstrates that impactful communities are possible on the app, with İrem İnceoglu and Yiğit Bahadır Kaya finding that LGBTI+ youth are able to construct "discrete bubbles" on TikTok that foster the expression of queer identity.[9] Additionally, Ellen Simpson and Bryan Semaan's 2020 study of LGBTQ+ users of TikTok finds that their respondents have discovered "a sense of community with other LGBTQ+ people they encountered on the app as manifest through their individual creativity and expression."[10] Their respondents attested to the community they encountered being a network they could "turn to for identity support and validation."[11]

Simpson and Semaan's interviews with TikTok users concluded in April 2020 at the beginning of the global COVID-19 pandemic. They infer that LGBTQ+ peoples' experiences on the app did not change following physical distancing orders. However, I would argue that the significance of the app to LGBTQ+ users during the pandemic would have increased. For queer people, the loss of physical spaces in which they can be in community with others is immense as these are the spaces in which queer people can shelter from and refuse heteronormative society's practices. For queer people holed up in their homes, with some potentially self-censoring because they now have to share space with parents or roommates they're not out to, TikTok becomes a portal to experience part of what they could be doing if they were free to be out in the world, in both senses of the term.[12]

This is not to say that TikTok is in itself a queer space. As George Chauncy has stated, "there is no queer space. There are only spaces put to queer uses."[13] On apps such as TikTok, this is possible through the "affordances" of social media, which refers to the possibilities for action when social media users interact with the mechanisms of platform design. Hanckel et al. (2019) have found that LGBTQ+ young people are using the functions of social media apps strategically so as to participate in queer-world-building.[14] Adding to their findings is Andre Cavalcante, who argues that the social media site Tumblr serves as Muñoz's "queer utopia" for LGBTQ+ youth.[15] I would argue that on Queer TikTok we can also see evidence of LGBTQ+ social media users generating "the specter of a 'queer utopia.'"

Queerness, as envisioned by Muñoz, is not yet here. "Queerness is an ideality," Muñoz argues, and while we may never touch queerness, "we can feel it as the warm illumination of a horizon imbued with potentiality."[16] In creating a queer utopia, one does not believe naively in perfection but rejects the here and now and insists on and strives for the potentiality of another world.[17] Potentiality, Muñoz explains, is different from possibility as the possible is linked to current material conditions; potentiality, on the other hand, does not exist in present things but in the horizon.[18] Queer utopia is perpetually immanent. It can never be arrived at; it only exists in our continual striving for a queer world that provides for one another.

The potentiality of a queer utopia can be found in everyday, quotidian acts, according to Muñoz. Acts of play, of performance, of connection with others—these are the moments in which we model glimpses for ways of being in the future. Central to Muñoz's concept of "queer utopia" is the transformative act of refusal, as per the Hegelian dialectic that he takes his cue from. More specifically, the refusal that Muñoz speaks of is the refusal of assimilationist moves toward incorporation into white, heteropatriarchal, imperial, capitalist society. Enacting this refusal is a performance that maps for audiences our repression, fragmentation, and alienation.[19] With this map, we can begin to chart pathways forward, not to a prescribed endpoint, but to a perpetual becoming in which we grow with and for one another.

I contend that queer TikTokers are participating in a long lineage of people who are working toward queer utopia, collectively forming the constellation that we can call Queer TikTok. With the work of queer creators on TikTok, there is a discernable desire or effort on their part to contribute to and strengthen the landscape of queer cultural texts, and to pass on advice for navigating queer identity, relationships, and community. As a loose collectivity, they are making breaks in heteronormative and homonormative thinking, and thereby providing glimpses into alternative queer modalities.

The Pandemic Made Me Gay(er)

A genre of Queer TikTok that is particularly notable for its illumination of a path toward a queer future are those TikToks that discuss or depict the loosening grip of heteronormativity in theirs and others lives as a result of the COVID-19 pandemic.[20] In fact, a number of people specifically identify their being on TikTok as a contributing factor to their queer revelations during the pandemic.[21] This genre is predominantly populated with queer women and non-binary people noting or imaginatively depicting that they or others have discovered during the pandemic that they are not attracted to men or less attracted than previously thought. These creators are utilizing the space of TikTok as a place in which they can announce, discuss, and revel in their explorations of gender and sexuality, hailing others from different publics with whom they can be in conversation and build community with.

TikTok creator @special_feel, for instance, says the following:

> I think it is so sad that we had to go through a global pandemic and mandatory quarantine wherein girls didn't have to perform their gender for anyone else and because of that, they realized that they were lesbians! (laughs).[22]

The creator theorizes that the observed trend of women and non-binary people realizing that they are not attracted to or interested in men is due to the necessity to pursue school or work from home during the pandemic. This shift meant that people were instead conducting their daily lives from the far more private sphere of their own home, reducing the number of public and bodily interactions with men or under the gaze of men for many women and non-binary people.

@grahsar agrees, identifying the hegemonic ideology that orders these public interactions as "compulsory heterosexuality," a concept introduced by essayist Adrienne Rich in 1980.[23] @kardashionion adds scholarly theory for this discussion, likely because, as noted in their caption, they have produced this video as a submission for a college course assignment.[24] They reference Judith Butler's "Performative Acts and Gender Constitution" (1988) in order to argue that the pandemic has "stagnated" the repeated performance of gender that is mandated by larger society.

Whilst their conclusion that people now only have to perform for themselves is questionable, considering the pervasive nature of gender and sexuality norms, their argument that this stagnation could prompt internal questioning of the kind of performances they are engaging in is merited. Potentially, people's isolation from the public outside their home could lead them to pursue other forms of gender performance that they have developed an interest in, with TikTok offering a fertile space to practice that performance and find others who model such gender and sexuality play. In offering this potential explanation for people's relatively sudden evolution of their gender and/or sexual identity, TikToks such as these chart out the map that Muñoz prescribes, in which our repression, fragmentation, and alienation are located. These TikToks are a form of consciousness-raising, naming for viewers the specificities of the similar experiences they have gone through and, for some, forecasting potential trajectories out of compulsory heterosexuality.

Complementing these discursive TikToks are those TikToks that are more theatrical, constructing representations of their own journey of queer evolution. These TikToks utilize remixed popular songs to construct a familiar narrative structure whilst their superimposed text and bodily movements personalize the narrative to convey their own story of discovering their gender and sexuality. Simpson and Semaan credit the use of specific audio clips for content creation as contributing to the supportive and welcoming nature of the LGBTQ+ TikTok community.[25] This is likely because creating content around a specific audio lends to others being able to recognize and replicate the identity performance they have observed, thereby affirming their place in a community of practice.

Creator Tanya Compas has overlaid their video with a remix of the song "Levitating" by Dua Lipa.[26] This song was very popular on TikTok in early 2021, with creators employing the call and response of the lyrics "you want me/I want you baby" to express desire toward something or someone.[27] A riff on this TikTok meme then developed wherein the response of "I want you baby" was edited out. By simply editing out the response of "I want you baby," the participant in this trend could instead use it to indicate refusal or a lack of desire for the object depicted, just as Compas does.

Compas sets the scene as "before the pandemic," with her past self-identifying as bisexual. She switches her clothing and the camera orientation to then pose as the undesirable entity of her video—cisgender men—and then lip-synchs to the lyrics "You want me" and uses the silence of what should be the response to indicate her lack of attraction to the original subject. This humorous diss is used by Compas to indicate that prior to the pandemic she had thought she was bisexual, but that she has since realized she "will never date a CIS man again."

Creator Joan has used a remixed version of the 2012 song "Gangnam Style" by PSY to convey the transformative process they have gone through during the pandemic.[28] The TikTok begins with audio of a person saying, "Oh my god he's dead? No!" signaling the death of the person that is described in the superimposed text—"a cis bi girl." While the text remains onscreen, Joan thrashes around their bedroom, their movements erratic and extremely fast as a result of video editing. The sound clip switches to the opening rhythm of the song "Gangnam Style" with the pulsing rhythm of the song leaving the audience in anticipation of the very familiar lyrics "oppa gangnam style."

This instrumental arc frames the narrative of the TikTok in a similar manner—just as we expect to hear the familiar, titular lyrics of

"Gangnam Style," we also expect the emergence of a new narrative subject to replace the cis bi girl who has metaphorically died. Sure enough, just as the anticipated lyrics play, Joan stops thrashing around and looks at the camera as new text that reads "non-binary lesbian" is superimposed on the frame. Thus, using the theatrics of a TikTok trend, the creator has been able to express the transformative experience that was discovering during the pandemic they were not a bisexual woman but a non-binary lesbian.

Both of these TikToks offer a performance of refusal and discovery that echoes Muñoz's description of queer utopia, in which the here and now is rejected in favor of the innovation of new queer futures. The very act of desiring involves a discontent with the organization of a current reality. To choose alterity is to reject one's present. And this rejection has enabled the two TikTok creators discussed here to come into their own, finding confidence and peace through the process, as depicted by their narrative arcs. In rejecting the heteronormative expectation that they, in being assigned female at birth, should be attracted to or desiring of men, the two TikTok creators reveal that they have been able to come into a better and more liberating understanding of who they are. These TikToks demonstrate for viewers the freedom that can come from listening to feelings of discontent with the way of things, inviting them to instead choose the future they desire.

In between the Trends: Archie Bongiovanni's Queer Utopia

From looking at popular trends on Queer TikTok, we can learn a lot about the queer potentialities in how TikTok is being used, but it is also important to zoom in on specific creators. In looking at the posts and experiences of individual creators, we can see between and beyond the trends and can thereby discover not only how the resulting discourse is extended out into differently impactful conversations, but also how the algorithm can debilitate the conversation. One queer TikTok creator whose work illuminates the potentialities of a queer utopia is Archie Bongiovanni. Archie is a 35-year-old genderqueer cartoonist, illustrator, and zine-maker in Minneapolis who uses TikTok to continue their pre-pandemic work of recommending sex toys. For those who may gain a greater understanding of their gender and sexuality through the pandemic or via TikTok, TikToks like Archie's may be the site of a more material investment in their queer future.

An example of Archie's work is a TikTok in which they respond to a commenter who asks whether there are strap-on sex toys that are pleasurable for the wearer without having to be inserted in the wearer's body.[29] Archie responds with a video of themself that is shot handheld from their mobile phone as they stroll and slightly dance down a tree-lined street walking their dog to a song by K-Pop band BTS. Archie has also superimposed text on this video that reads, "Yes! It sounds like ur looking for something that stays outside of the bod, here are my ideas! Lmk urs in the comments" and then proceeds to provide recommendations for this kind of sex toy in text that is superimposed on the subsequent frames of their video.

This video is a gleeful offering from a queer creator to assist their digital neighbors. In their video, Archie uses casual language and a public setting, demonstrating that their account is a place to discuss the topic of queer sex and pleasure openly and without any shame. Their performance in this video is a refusal of the dictates of comportment in public space, reclaiming public space to be the site where queer celebration and discussion can take place. Additionally, in choosing to shoot their video as they go about their day, Archie has created a point of connection to their viewer, who can feel as though they are receiving advice from a trusted friend. It feels especially important to see such a performance during COVID times, with queer spaces at risk due to business closures and physical distancing requirements.

In creating this space of interpersonal intimacy, Archie is better able to provide information that can aid their viewers in their queer sex goals. The information that they provide is detailed and considers various goals or concerns that the commenter might have, such as comfort and maximizing pleasure. In providing such a service, Archie demonstrates a commitment to realizing the vision of queer futurity that Muñoz describes—one that is "all about desire."[30] Archie has taken the opportunity to configure a space that was not made specifically with queer people in mind in order to create new openings to a queer potentiality. Additionally, Archie destabilizes the homonormative primacy of the cisgender, able-bodied gay man by producing and sharing resources that specifically attend to the experiences of people in LGBTQ+ communities who are non-binary and/or disabled, to name just a couple of the experiences and identities that are spoken to on their page.

This is likely to be the reason that Archie faces considerable censorship on the app.[31] Archie has had many of their TikToks taken down, and in May 2021, their account was deleted, cutting them off from a huge audience they had built for interaction and to sustain their small business. After two days of raising awareness of their situation and drumming up some support, the account was returned to Archie but the incident is illustrative of the vulnerable position that queer and other marginalized creators are in on social media platforms like Tik-Tok. Simpson and Semaan document that many of their research participants have experienced or observed situations similar to that of Archie's.[32]

Black TikTok creators in particular have been working hard to expose TikTok's discriminatory algorithm.[33] Non-binary creator Ryan Ken has spoken out on Twitter about the removal of one of their videos satirizing cis straight male comedy for what TikTok deemed hate speech violations. Ken calls TikTok a "wild case study of how we build bias into our technologies" and warns that "if enough people choose to say 'Can I speak to a manager?' to an algorithm, someone's entire livelihood can be cut off."[34] Here, Ken is referring to the practice in which TikTok users will report content as violating TikTok's community guidelines in order to get it removed, an issue that Simpson and Semaan noted as prevalent for queer TikTok creators.[35]

In Archie's case, along with other queer content creators on TikTok, TikTok's community guideline against the posting of "sexually explicit content" is usually cited as the reason for their content removal. Much like the Tumblr ban on sexually explicit content in 2017, this community guideline can be and is wielded to suppress LGBTQ+ content.[36] This policy disappointed queer Tumblr users and drove many people away from the app.[37] In fact, Simpson and Semaan's study of LGBTQ+ TikTok users found that some of their participants had moved away from Tumblr and toward other social media spaces like TikTok for exactly this reason.[38] It remains to be seen how TikTok's implementation of a similar policy, as well as its anti-Black policies, will impact the pursuit of queer utopia on the app.

Conclusion

Queer utopia, as described by Muñoz, is an evolving innovation in which the future is designed and redesigned based off of the cues of our past and the rejection of the constraints of our present. It is a creative force that strides ahead of the inertia imposed by a pragmatic homonormative politics. During the pandemic, queer people have utilized the space of TikTok for a generative play through refusal and creation, seizing the opportunity for public yet intimate performance in order to come into themselves and build community.

For queer women and non-binary people, this journey has been one of great transformation, breaking down the hold of heteronormativity and cisnormativity on their lives. Queer women and non-binary

TikTok creators are developing their own theories of how exactly this transformation has come about and what role both TikTok and the pandemic has played in the process. Further research on these experiences and theories is required so as to better understand queer women and non-binary people's use of social media technology, as well as what this usage reveals about the functioning of the cis heteropatriarchal system.

The continued viability of TikTok for efforts toward queer utopia is yet to be determined, with TikTok's interpretation and implementation of conduct violation policy continually falling on the side of the white supremacist heteropatriarchy. Nevertheless, the methods developed by creators on the app to create cultural texts and build community are powerful and also show signs of being translated into in-person strategies. As of this writing, I am aware of three pop-ups or meet-ups organized by queer/lesbian creators on TikTok that have occurred in 2021 in cities such as Los Angeles, Austin, and Denver.[39] To better understand our directions toward queer utopia, future scholarship will need to bear witness to community-building methods on the app and as they make their way out into additional spaces.

Notes

1 Note: An earlier version of this research, titled ""Do you want to form an alliance with me?": Queer Techno-Corporeal Communities on TikTok during COVID-19," was presented at the Annual Meeting of the Cultural Studies Association 2021 on June 12, 2021.
  Alayna Joy (@missfenderr), "Thank god for the older wiser gays #babygay #lgbt #lgbtq #queer #wlw," TikTok, September 25, 2020, https://vm.tiktok.com/ZMRrXUd1j/
2 Kristen D. Krause, "Implications of the COVID-19 Pandemic on LGBTQ Communities," *Journal of Public Health Management and Practice* 27, no. 1 (January/February 2021): S69; Jorge Gato, Daniela Leal, and Daniel Seabra, "When Home Is Not a Safe Haven: Effects of the COVID-19 Pandemic on LGBTQ Adolescents and Young Adults in Portugal," *PSICOLOGIA* 34, no. 2 (2020): 9.
3 Jack Halberstam, *In a Queer Time and Place: Transgender Bodies, Subcultural Lives* (New York: New York University Press, 2005), 12.
4 Maxine Wolfe, "Invisible Women in Invisible Places: Lesbians, Lesbian Bars, and the Social Production of People/Environment Relationships," *Architecture & Comportement/ Architecture & Behaviour* 8, no. 2 (1992): 147; Christina B. Hanhardt, *Safe Space: Gay Neighborhood History and the Politics of Violence* (Durham, NC: Duke University Press, 2013).
5 Ivan Pereira, "NYPD Clashes with Protesters during Pride Rally on Anniversary of Stonewall Riots," *ABC News* June 30, 2020, https://abcnews.go.com/US/nypd-clashes-protesters-pride-rally-anniversary-stonewall-riots/story?id=71510651

6 Melanie Kennedy, "'If the Rise of the TikTok Dance and E-girl Aesthetic Has Taught us Anything, It's That Teenage Girls Rule the Internet Right Now': Tik Tok Celebrity, Girls and the Coronavirus Crisis," *European Journal of Cultural Studies* 23, no. 6 (2020): 2.

7 Diana Zulli and David James Zulli, "Extending the Internet Meme: Conceptualizing Technological Mimesis and Imitation Publics on the TikTok Platform," *New Media & Society* (2020): 1.

8 Ibid., 12.

9 İrem İnceoglu and Yiğit Bahadır Kaya, "Tiktokivism: Grouping of LGBTI+ Youth on TikTok's Semi-Discrete Environments," paper presented at *TikTok Cultures: TikTok and Social Movements*, September 20, 2021.

10 Ellen Simpson and Bryan Semaan, "For You, or For "You"?: Everyday LGBTQ+ Encounters with TikTok," *Proceedings of the ACM on Human-Computer Interaction* 4, CSCW3, Article 252 (December 2020): 17.

11 Ibid., 17–18.

12 Malavika Kannan, "The Pandemic Hit LGBTQ Youth Hard. Many Turned to TikTok," *San Francisco Chronicle*, June 13, 2021, https://www.sfchronicle.com/local/article/The-pandemic-hit-LGBTQ-youth-hard-Many-turned-to-16242541.php.

13 George Chauncey, "Privacy Could Only Be Had in Public: Gay Uses of the Streets," in *Stud: Architectures of Masculinity*, ed. Joel Sanders (New York: Princeton Architectural Press, 1996), 224.

14 Benjamin Hanckel, Son Vivienne, Paul Byron, Brady Robards, and Brendan Churchill, "'That's Not Necessarily for Them': LGBTIQ+ Young People, Social Media Affordances and Identity Curation," *Media, Culture & Society* 41, no. 8 (2019): 1275.

15 Andre Cavalcante, "Tumbling into Queer Utopias and Vortexes: Experiences of LGBTQ Social Media Users on Tumblr," *Journal of Homosexuality* 66, no. 12 (2019): 1715–1735.

16 Jose Esteban Muñoz, *Cruising Utopia: The Then and There of Queer Futurity* (New York: New York University Press, 2009), 1.

17 Ibid., 1; 10.

18 Ibid., 99.

19 Ibid., 55.

20 See Julia Mastroianni, "How the Pandemic Led These People to Come out as Queer and Non-Binary," *Now Toronto,* December 24, 2020, https://nowtoronto.com/lifestyle/how-pandemic-led-these-people-to-come-out-queer-and-non-binary; Anna Iovine, "The Pandemic Offered a Unique Chance to Come out as Queer," *Mashable,* March 22, 2021, https://mashable.com/article/covid-coming-out-queer-lgbtq-pandemic

21 Ibid.

22 Posted by @special_feel in 2020, whose account was suspended in June 2021.

23 grahsar (@grahsar7), "Quarantine Is Good for Some Things #wlw #queer #lgbtq," TikTok, November 19, 2020, vm.tiktok.com/ZMdogs2EH/.

24 Gsfs 289 final project (@kardashionion), "tap to pause and read! GSFS 289 final project Butler, Judith. "Performative Acts and Gender Constitution" in Feminist Theory Reader," TikTok, December 1, 2020.

25 Simpson and Semaan, "For You, or For "You"?" 18.

26 Tanya Compas (@tanyacompas), "Top Lad and Massive Gay. All It Means Is I'm Tanya and Don't Date CIS Men Anymore #lgbttiktok #uklgbt #GARNIERMASKMOMENT #fyp #foryoupage," TikTok, May 7, 2021, vm.tiktok.com/ZMdopHVeT/.

27 Nicholas Reimann, "How TikTok Keeps Dua Lipa 'Levitating' at the Top of the Charts," *Forbes*, May 17, 2021, https://www.forbes.com/sites/nicholasreimann/2021/05/14/how-tiktok-keeps-dua-lipa-levitating-at-the-top-of-the-charts/?sh=a25981928bab.

28 Joan (@frogandtoadaregay), "the pandemic bi girl to nb lesbian industrial complex #wlw #sapphic #lgbtq," TikTok, April 7, 2021, vm.tiktok.com/ZMdop97J1/.

29 Archie (@grease_bat), "good morning #strapped #strapon #fyp #foryoupage #pegtok #lgbt #queer #lgbtq #foryou," *TikTok*, September 11, 2020, https://vm.tiktok.com/ZMRSmECQJ/.

30 Muñoz, *Cruising Utopia: The Then and There of Queer Futurity*, 30.

31 Umberto Bacchi, "TikTok apologises for censoring LGBT+ content," *Reuters*, September 22, 2020, https://www.reuters.com/article/britain-tech-lgbt/tiktok-apologises-for-censoring-lgbt-content-idUSL5N2GJ459.

32 Simpson and Semaan, "For You, or For "You"?" 22.

33 See Taiyler Simone Mitchell, "Black Creators Say TikTok's Algorithm Fosters a 'consistent undertone of anti-Blackness.' Here's how the app has responded," *Insider*, August 24, 2021, https://www.insider.com/a-timeline-of-allegations-that-tiktok-censored-black-creators-2021-7; Conor Murray, "TikTok Algorithm Error Sparks Allegations of Racial Bias," *NBC News*, July 9, 2021, https://www.nbcnews.com/news/us-news/tiktok-algorithm-prevents-user-declaring-support-black-lives-matter-n1273413.

34 Ryan Ken (they/them) (@Ryan_Ken_Acts), "TikTok (@tiktok_us) Removed This Video for "hate speech" Violations. That Site a Wild Case Study of How We Build Bias into Our Technologies. And the way Black Creators Shape Trends on the Platform..." Twitter, July 7, 2021, https://twitter.com/Ryan_Ken_Acts/status/1412761983120809987.

35 Simpson and Semaan, "For You, or For "You"?" 22.

36 Cavalcante, "Tumbling into Queer Utopias and Vortexes: Experiences of LGBTQ Social Media Users on Tumblr," 1732; Stefanie Duguay, "Why Tumblr's Ban on Adult Content Is Bad for LGBTQ Youth," *The Conversation*, December 7, 2018, https://theconversation.com/why-tumblrs-ban-on-adult-content-is-bad-for-lgbtq-youth-108215.

37 Paige Leskin, "A Year after Tumblr's Porn Ban, Some Users Are Struggling to Rebuild Their Communities and Sense of Belonging," *Business Insider Australia*, December 21, 2019, https://www.businessinsider.com.au/tumblr-porn-ban-nsfw-flagged-reactions-fandom-art-erotica-communities-2019-8?r=US&IR=T.

38 Simpson and Semaan, "For You, or For "You"?" 10.

39 Caitlin Hernández, "Will This New Queer Space Change Lesbian Nightlife in Los Angeles?" *USA Today*, August 5, 2021, https://www.usatoday.com/story/life/2021/08/05/hot-donnas-clubhouse-change-los-angeles-lesbian-nightlife/5502534001/; Abby (@double.aye), "Calling Austin TX le$beans (gays & allys) join us at Zilker Park this Sunday March 30 from 3–7pm for Hot Gay Summer #lesbiansoftiktok #lgbtq #pride," *TikTok*, May 25, 2021, https://vm.tiktok.com/ZMRB8njAW/; Van (@simply_van), "Our Third CO Queer TikTok Meet Up! #lgbt #lgbtfriends #colorado #denver #lgbtcolorado #coqueertiktokgroup," TikTok, June 25, 2021, https://vm.tiktok.com/ZMRB8njAW/.

7   Trans TikTok

Sharing Information and Forming Community

Elle Rochford and Zachary D. Palmer

User 1 – "[H]ow did you get your family to support you my family hated me because of it (closed eyes frown emoji)"
User 2 – "You've got a big global family baby lean on us you are loved and supported..."
User 3 – "honey im your family, the trans community are your family and we all love you very much"

The above quotes are pulled from the comment section of Ted Kincaid's[1] viral TikTok on parenting as a trans man.[2] In the video, Kincaid responds to a commenter who claims Kincaid's children deserve pity as they must be incredibly confused. Kincaid videos himself asking his children a series of basic questions about who he is, who he is to them, and what it means to be trans. His children respond simply and as if they are bored by the conversation. Commenters leave messages of support or anger. Interactions such as this one suggest that TikTok can be a critical site for community, a space where users support each other and act as an extended, chosen family. However, in our study of 450 videos and comments, we found very few exchanges like the one above. The potential for trans TikTok to be a community-building space drew us to the platform, but ultimately the structure of the platform and the reward system for content discourages nuanced conversations and sustained exchanges of solidarity and support.

The Internet has long been a space for trans people to form community, facilitating connections that geography and social stigma might otherwise prevent. In the early days of the Internet, trans people connected with one another in chatrooms and shared resources and explored their identities through GeoCities websites.[3] Later, YouTube and Tumblr became the dominant online spaces for the transgender community, with some scholars referring to Tumblr as a "trans technology," due to its characteristics of "multiplicity, fluidity, and

DOI: 10.4324/9781003280705-10

ambiguity."[4] Both YouTube and Tumblr were platforms for trans discourse through comments and re-blogging, in which users shared others' posts and could add their own commentary. On Tumblr, popular hashtags such as #ftm, #mtf, and #trans* provided a repository of the conversations on these topics and a "safe space" for education, self-expression, and connection. On YouTube, personal transition vlogs became their own genre, with their "talking head"[5] style facilitating a sense of intimacy and community while sharing "embodied trans knowledges"[6] about the transition process.

Tumblr has since been abandoned by the trans community (and many others) due to bans on adult content that were often selectively used to police trans content.[7] YouTube has also declined in popularity, with TikTok now the ascendant social media platform. TikTok estimates it will have over 70 million active users in 2021 in the United States alone.[8] Trans TikTok, unlike YouTube and Tumblr, is distributed overwhelmingly to cis users. TikTok offers financial and social opportunities for trans creators, but also offers cis audiences new insights into the lived experiences of trans people. TikTok, as compared to Instagram and YouTube, favors diversity and relatability which expands *who* can be a top influencer and have the potential to earn millions.[9] This is important as trans people frequently experience employment discrimination especially if they belong to a marginalized racial group.[10] Moreover, for many cis people, social media may be their only or first window into the lives of trans people. Cis users can consume trans content on their own terms from the comfort and safety of their phones.

There is certainly trans content on TikTok and a large trans user base, but how do users create community and what does this community look like? If Tumblr was a "trans technology," how might we characterize TikTok with its extremely short videos and notorious (and inscrutable) algorithm? Recent work on "TransTok" celebrates the revolutionary acts of trans creators and is beginning to explore trans comedy and community.[11] We add to this discussion by unpacking the possibilities and limitations of community on TikTok. In this chapter, we examine the trans community on TikTok through content analysis of posts and associated comments from eight trans influencers as well as posts from the "trans" hashtag. We find that, in part due to the structure of the TikTok algorithm and what it rewards, many trans videos are geared toward cisgender audiences. Additionally, since controversy drives engagement, trans creators utilizing transphobic humor or directly responding to transphobic trolls are often the most popular videos. Thus, TikTok facilitates trans *content* but rarely trans *community.* Instead, the goal for many trans creators appears to be about affirmation, engagement, and fun.

Data and Methods

To explore the trans community on TikTok, we performed a content analysis as it is well suited to analyzing visual data as well as text.[12] We collected and analyzed 450 posts from eight influencers who identify as trans or non-binary and the top posts using the hashtag "trans." We began data collection on May 7, 2021 and collected the 50 most recent publicly available posts from each influencer. We also collected and analyzed the first ten comments on each post, as well as the first ten replies to each of those ten comments. Here, "first" refers to the order in which the comments are listed when opened by the researcher. Comments and replies are not necessarily displayed chronologically or by popularity. It appears the algorithm partially randomizes the order (for instance, opening the comments for the same video may result in different top comments). It seems priority is given to comments by verified users, popular comments, and comments the creator replies to; however, this is not consistent. For each comment and post, we collected metadata such as the post's username, date, number of likes, number of comments/replies, caption, etc. Users were given pseudonyms.

We sought variation in our sample regarding gender identity by selecting a mix of trans men, trans women, and non-binary/genderqueer users. Sampling the "trans" hashtag allows us a broad overview of the types of users engaging in conversation about trans identity and content that are created under the hashtag. Our research pays close attention to racial identity both in our sampling and analysis. We also include users with a variety of followers, though all can be characterized as "meso" or "macro" level influencers—that is, they have greater than 10,000 or 1 million followers, respectively.[13] See Table 1 for a description of our cases, including demographics based on user's self-descriptions (either in their videos or bios) (Table 7.1).

To analyze our data, we use comprehensive memoing. Memoing in qualitative work refers to the practice of taking detailed and systematic notes which allow researchers to produce intellectual capital and increase abstract thinking and the connection of concepts.[14] We began with descriptive memoing, which involves taking detailed notes describing the content. We then moved to thematic memoing examining themes, motifs, symbols, and common ideas that appeared in both the raw data and within our descriptive memos. Continuous memoing

Table 7.1 Demographics and data

Case (pseudonyms)	Gender identity	Race/ethnicity	#likes	#followers
Charlie	Non-binary	Black	989.5K	49.2K
Coco	Trans femme	AAPI/Latina	244.6M	14.1M
Jason	Trans masc	White	8.4M	451.1K
Kai	Non-binary	White	35M	643.8K
Ray	Trans masc	Black	2.9M	178.9K
Sammy	Trans masc	White	49M	1.9M
Scarlett	Trans femme	Black	7M	532.7K
Tara	Trans femme	AAPI	48M	776.4K
Hashtag	N/A	N/A	19.4B views	N/A

and meta-memoing (to memo about memoing) results in new codes, themes, and coding strategies.[15] By utilizing repeated memoing, we were able to isolate three key themes: the centering of cis audiences, the crucial role of transphobia in boosting content and creators, and the focus on individual goals versus community-building.

Characterizing Trans TikTok

YouTube was the first space in which trans people widely produced and consumed video content, with transition videos being the main type of content in that space.[16] In these videos, people documented their physical and social transitions and engaged in communities of support with other trans people. The videos by trans creators on Tik-Tok, however, are of a very different nature and appeared to fulfill a very different purpose. Instead of a singular, specific genre of trans videos, TikTok content tends to primarily conform to the conventions of TikTok while potentially putting a trans spin on popular trends such as "glow-up" videos (in which users trace a transformation over time to being more conventionally attractive), lip-syncs, make-up tutorials, and comedy sketches.

Some creators make content that focuses on their trans identities, such as Jason, who makes humorous videos about being a trans man and his relationship with his trans girlfriend. Coco's "thirst trap" videos frequently highlight the fact that she is trans, and she often includes jokes about being "born a boy" or "dude." Sammy's content often directly discusses his experiences as a trans man who has given birth. For others, however, being trans is something that remains in the background, sometimes quite literally. For example, Tara primarily records dancing and lip-sync videos, but does so with a large trans flag in the background. Similarly, Charlie's content focuses on comedy skits where they play characters of all genders and, while their skits often focus on being queer or gay, they do not explicitly discuss their gender identity beyond the pronouns in their bio.

As opposed to the directly educational content often found in You-Tube transition videos, such as discussing the process of starting hormone replacement therapy, the TikToks we analyze only indirectly include educational information—typically communicating through humor. For instance, Scarlett pokes fun at the difficulties of dating while trans. Rarely are these videos in conversation with others within the community, beyond "duet" videos where users record a video, often involving singing, dancing, or lip synching, that runs simultaneously alongside a video from another user. These duet videos, however, are rarely (if ever) related to being trans. Instead of being for education or connection, the purpose of many of these videos primarily seems to be affirmation and fun. Exchanges of support like the one that opens this chapter are not common. Conversations in the comments are often difficult to follow. Replies are nested but users may comment responses starting new threads or reply to the wrong comment. Comments and replies are not presented by like or chronologically so users new to the comment section may respond to something that had already been resolved or misunderstand the comment they were responding to. Nuanced conversations are all but impossible and misunderstandings quickly escalate, but misunderstandings drive engagement so there is little incentive for TikTok to redesign.

A Window for Cis People into Trans Worlds

User 1 – "[S]aying you can't tell isn't a compliment so don't say that guys"

User 2 – "[O]bviously there's nothing wrong with being trans LOL. I mean I can't rly say what is and isn't offensive bc I'm not trans but I think ppl mean that for some ppl you can definitely tell, but I think that the majority of trans people have the same goal- to look like their destined gender!"

User 3 – "Huh??? I had a friend who was trans and he loved when people told him that. They're just saying they couldn't tell that he isn't cis"

The above exchange takes place in the comments of Deforestation's comedy video. In the video, he uses a trending sound, "my body different," to explain to an imagined woman why he can't "hook up" right now. Deforestation is a conventionally attractive man and the video receives a number of comments from users shocked he was trans. Some users attempt to educate cis users on why their "compliments" may be offensive. Trans influencers with the highest follower counts can achieve such large amounts of followers in part because they are able to appeal to cis users. It is statistically unlikely that the majority of Coco's 14.1 million followers are also transgender. For those invested in generating engagement and large audiences, appealing to cis users is a necessity. In fact, much of the content we analyze seems designed for cis audiences with limited knowledge of the LGBTQ+ community rather than trans or queer people. And, based on the comments, many of the consumers of trans TikTokers' videos are cisgender. Though it is not always possible to distinguish users' identities based on their comments, many identify themselves as cis as a lead-in to questions about the trans experience or thanking the creator for educating them. For instance, "You are making such an important contribution to your whole movement," one user comments on Jason's post from Trans Day of Remembrance, "you've taken a challenging situation and turned it into something really great." Allies regularly thank creators for being "inspirational," and for sharing their stories. Others comment asking for clarification of commonly used terms in the trans community like "dead name" and "stealth," discouraging the use of in-group language without definitions.

It is clear that trans TikTok is a window into trans culture and experience for some cis people, a way of coming into contact with the "other," either as a curious, well-intentioned ally or a gawking troll. The overwhelming majority of videos from trans creators we analyze have at least one comment intentionally misgendering them (for instance "that's actually a guy") or expressing transphobic beliefs ("u can't change ur gender bro"). Allies often flood to correct instances of misgendering and to chastise transphobes. A common exchange, particularly on posts by trans women, involves the use of asterisks and pronouns (for example, *he). A troll will comment an asterisk with incorrect pronouns "correcting" a user or the creator's caption. Fans of the account will then respond with dozens of counter corrections, which often earn more "likes" compared to the original transphobic comment. These exchanges allow cis users to visibly assert themselves as allies.

This is not to say that trans videos do not attract trans viewers. Many comments are from other trans people identifying with creator's content and answering questions from cis people. However, we observe few conversations between creators and trans followers specifically discussing trans issues—something that one might expect looking for community structured around shared trans identity and in contrast to other online trans communities. Macro influencers like Sammy and Coco occasionally reply to verified users and other influencers, but rarely reply to fan comments. Other creators, particularly Charlie and Kai, make videos specifically for queer audiences. Both focus on comedy sketches, often mocking how cis and straight people view queer people. For example, in one sketch, Charlie pretends to be a gay boom operator watching a straight actor pretend to be gay, the ridiculousness of the straight actor overly relying on gay stereotypes being the butt of the joke. Perhaps tellingly, Charlie has one of the lowest number of followers, suggesting that making content that centers queer perspectives may not generate as much popularity as that which caters to cis audiences.

Transphobia as a Driver of Engagement

USER 1 – "it's a guy"

USER 2 – "She's a girl- stay mad bestie"

USER 1 – "lol sure bud I'm pretty sure if I said I was a girl I would still be a guy"

USER 2 – "Just say ur insecure and go"

Above is an example of trolling content from one of Tara's TikToks. The structure and flow of TikTok, as well as what the algorithm rewards, means that certain types of trans creators gain large audiences. TikTok measures not just what the audience likes, but what they watch and interact with. Sharing a video (even if it is just to mock in a group chat) or skipping over a video before a second has elapsed provides meaningful data points to the algorithm. TikTok therefore, in many ways, measures attention.[17] As a result, confusing, chaotic, and/or eye-catching TikToks have a better chance of being viewed fully and by more people. As users cannot "dislike" videos, negative feedback manifests through ratios (when a post has far more shares and comments than likes) and hate comments, both of which encourage the algorithm to circulate the video more widely. Therefore, controversy generates engagement.

Viral fame is exceedingly hard to predict, but many users will attempt to either recreate a successful post (either one of their own or another users) or they will purposefully post inflammatory messages. Political duets where a user responds and shames the views of another user are routinely used as a pathway to viral fame.[18] The most popular users are not always the most beloved, but rather those most willing to engage in controversy. Offline controversies can also translate to TikTok engagement. Coco's comment sections, for instance, are often flooded with users calling her out for anti-Black discrimination that occur on other platforms. One user, Queen Cat called out Coco's fans commenting, "Um excuse me? You support that her being disrespectful to cultures and changing her skin tone then joking about it on Twitter. Blackfishing isn't cool." Users commenting on Coco's fashion or dance videos asking her about racist incidents or her use of the n-word perhaps unknowingly boost her videos' circulation. Coco also collaborates frequently with cis men fueling speculations and dating rumors. "Stans" of these male influencers or those who "ship" the men with a different influencer frequently leave transphobic messages discouraging the pair. On one video of Coco with a famous influencer, commenters argue they could never date because the man was straight and Coco was trans, "Nope that's not how it works I support trans but nope." Users reply arguing back and forth about trans/cis relationships and sexual orientations.

In terms of trans TikTok, transphobia is a large driver of controversy and, therefore, engagement. Though neither party would likely think of it this way, there is an almost symbiotic relationship between transphobic trolls and trans content creators. The TikTok algorithm funnels users into content silos based upon the videos with which they interact, even if their interaction consists of hate comments. If a trans influencer posts a video and a troll comments a transphobic insult, the troll will be given more trans content while the original video will be circulated to more users similar to the troll. This can create a vicious cycle of transphobic users who are increasingly frustrated by the amount of trans content they are seeing.

However, trans users often give transphobic trolls attention by making videos directly responding to their comments. In turn, these "clap back" videos generate massive amounts of engagement, both in the form of support from allies and further attacks from trolls. For example, one of Ray's most popular videos is one in which he is dancing to music with his shirt off, with "just because you had surgeries doesn't mean you're a man now" on the screen. His facial expression, casual attitude, and muscular physique in the video all suggest the ridiculousness of this comment and how little it mattered to him. This garnered 30.5K likes and 427 comments, much more than many of his other videos. Tara's response to transphobes play up her femininity and sexuality, a direct dare to the viewer to question their assessment of her gender (and, perhaps, their anxiety at being attracted to her). In one video, she displays a screenshot of a comment in which someone calls her a man, only to come onto the screen in a skimpy schoolgirl outfit, makeup, and a blonde wig, playing with her hair and dancing for the camera with the text "he's not available anymore;)." In another video, user Eve posts a screenshot of middle-aged women ranting about how Eve will never be a "real woman." Eve dances in a string bikini while emphasizing the ways she (Eve) is conventionally more attractive than the transphobic commenter. Her video received over two million likes but also dozens of disparaging comments about how Eve uses plastic surgery and makeup but was still a "he." Being able to make trolls look foolish or demonstrate that one did not care about their opinion, sometimes by engaging in gendered and sexual displays, is therefore an important driver of engagement for many trans creators. This does not discount the hurtful or offensive nature of trolls, only that Tik-Tok's algorithm rewards controversy and so such creators can strategically derive some benefit from and otherwise potentially painful online interaction.

Other trans creators directly play into transphobic tropes for humor, either subverting transphobia or utilizing it as a driver of views and likes. Trans women shifting into a deep voice or joking about the size of their penises is common in the #trans videos. Others play with the idea of trans women as "traps," "tricking" heterosexual men into sexual encounters. While these types of videos can be interpreted as internalized transphobia, contextualizing them within many creators' larger bodies of work suggests that they are tongue-in-cheek and self-aware. The popularity of such videos can lead to monetization and other financial and social opportunities for users such as promotions and free products to review. Creators appear to be strategic and savvy, particularly those with large follower counts who clearly understand on some level how to exploit the algorithm.

Does Trans Content Translate to Trans Community?

While most of the creators we look at position themselves as influencers rather than community-builders, there are some notable exceptions. Kai's videos appear to primarily attract a young, queer audience, and the goal of Kai's page appears to be primarily to promote their LGBTQ+ club in Discord, a messaging app that facilitates online communities. Discord allows groups to chat in various channels which hosts can moderate or restrict. For instance, a caption on one of their comedy skit videos reads, "[rainbow flag emoji] join our LGBTQ+ club or sponsor a teen! #lgbtq #lgbt #comedy #mom #funny." In this way, Kai connects with their viewers, grabs their attention through their videos, and funnels that viewership into their club. Thus, TikTok is a site of community-building for Kai and their followers, though it is more where community is promoted and recruited. Though discussions occur within the comments of the videos, it is clear that the primary community exists in a separate online space (Discord).

It is possible that the trans community flourishes on TikTok, though it does not appear to do so on the pages of high-profile influencers or the trans hashtag. It is possible that due to the increasing number of physical and digital spaces for community, TikTok does not *need* to be a community-building space. The number of trans influencers celebrating personal successes or creating content beyond educational materials is perhaps a sign that trans creators have more freedom to create. Trans influencers may reference or even center their gender identities but they are also allowed identities beyond their gender—style icons, dancers, comedians, parents, gossip magnets, and actors. Transphobia and trolls are obviously still a significant barrier to trans people on- and offline, but the number of trans influencers and the popularity of trans content on TikTok suggests that there is also a growing number of cis people who are aware of and support trans people. The "trans" hashtag has amassed 19.4 *billion* views and the videos in our study earned millions of likes. The top 50 videos were of trans or queer creators or close allies such as parents or educators (not trolls or transphobes using the hashtag) and these videos overwhelmingly celebrate trans identities.

TikTok can be a tricky platform for meaningful discourse. The platform has little reason to facilitate communication building in the comments as misunderstandings and disagreements fuel engagement. Users are also incentivized to engage with trolls and controversies. However, many trans users are thriving on TikTok. The platform dramatically increases the visibility of trans and non-binary people. Cis users have seemingly endless access to trans' stories, content, and creators. Users attempt to educate each other in the comments and engage in discussions about LGBTQ+ terms, issues, and identities. Creators can subvert or utilize transphobia to elevate their accounts and earn social and financial rewards. While the platform mirrors gender, racial, and other inequalities by favoring thin, athletic, white, conventionally attractive creators, the size of the platform seemingly provides space for people of all gender expressions to innovate and create.

Acknowledgments

The authors would like to thank artists and TikTokers Gracie Martin and Jesse Cale for their insights into the app.

Notes

1 Ted Kincaid is a pseudonym; all users are given pseudonyms.
2 Kincaid's video using the hashtag "trans" earned 1.7 million likes and more than 7,000 comments and replies.
3 Avery Dame-Griff, "How the Bulletin Board Systems, Email Lists and Geocities Pages of the Early Internet Created a Place for Trans Youth to Find One Another and EXPLORE Coming Out," *The Conversation*, May 25, 2021, theconversation.com/how-the-bulletin-board-systems-email-lists-and-geocities-pages-of-the-early-internet-created-a-place-for-trans-youth-to-find-one-another-and-explore-coming-out-159681.
4 Oliver L. Haimson, Avery Dame-Griff, Elias Capello, and Zahari Richter, "Tumblr Was a Trans Technology: The Meaning, Importance, History, and Future of Trans Technologies," *Feminist Media Studies* 21, no. 3 (2019): 345–361.
5 Laura Horak, "Trans on YouTube: Intimacy, Visibility, Temporality," *Transgender Studies Quarterly* 1, no. 4 (2014): 572–585.
6 Tobias Raun, "Video Blogging as a Vehicle of Transformation: Exploring the Intersection between Trans Identity and Information Technology," *International Journal of Cultural Studies* 18, no. 3 (2015): 365–378.
7 Hamison et al., "Tumblr Was a Trans Technology."
8 https://www.statista.com/statistics/1100836/number-of-us-tiktok-users/
9 Crystal Abidin, "Mapping Internet Celebrity on TikTok: Exploring Attention Economies and Visibility Labours," *Cultural Science Journal* 12, no. 1 (2021): 77–103.
10 Mario I. Suárez, Guadalupe Marquez-Velarde, Christy Glass, and Gabe H. Miller, "Cis-Normativity at Work: Exploring Discrimination against US Trans Workers," *Gender in Management*, No. ahead-of-print (2020): 1–16. https://doi.org/10.1108/GM-06-2020-0201
11 Timmins, Benjamin and Nicholas-Brie Guarriello, "Gender? I Hardly Know Her: "TransTok" and TikTok's Gender-Conscious Communities," *TikTok and Social Movements*, September 20, 2021, TikTok Cultures Research Network.
12 Maggi Salvin-Baden and Claire Howell Major, *Qualitative Research: The Essential Guide to Theory and Practice* (Philadelphia: Routledge, 2013).
13 Sophie C. Boerman, "The Effects of the Standardized Instagram Disclosure for Micro- and Meso- Influencers," *Computers in Human Behavior* 103 (2020): 199–207.
14 Kathy Charmaz, *Constructing Grounded Theory: A Practical Guide through Qualitative Analysis* (London: Sage, 2006), 109–137; Adele E. Clarke, *Situational Analysis: Grounded Theory after the Postmodern Turn* (London: Sage, 2005), 28.
15 Melanie Birks, Ysanne Chapman, and Karen Francis, "Memoing in Qualitative Research: Probing Data and Processes," *Journal of Nursing Research* 13 (2007): 68–75.
16 Horak, "Trans on YouTube," 572–585.
17 Abidin, "Mapping Internet Celebrity on TikTok," 81–85.
18 Ibid., 77–103.

Section Three
TikTok (Sub)Cultures

8   Hocus-Pocus
WitchTok Education for Baby Witches

Jane Barnette

Can magical spells be taught through the medium of video? If Witch-Tok is any indication, millions of users believe they can learn witchcraft through TikTok, a realization that dawned on the wider public after reports circulated in July 2020 that "baby witches" wanted to hex the moon. Aside from the fact that cursing an entire natural satellite is absurd, within most witch belief systems, it would also be extremely dangerous. Responses to poorly planned or executed magical attempts like these quickly followed, with more experienced witches offering advice as well as warnings to assert community norms, all under the hashtag #WitchTok.

A year later, there are numerous subcultures within WitchTok, ranging from BabyWitchTok to CrystalTok to BlackWitchTok, allowing users to curate their viewing and posting even further, while highlighting the variety of methods for practicing witchcraft. While several posts include "witch" in their hashtag with the goal of undermining or spoofing witchy behavior, at least as many appear to be made earnestly, by creators who already identify as witches.

That said, personal curation is designed to be increasingly satisfying the more users interact with TikTok: the app defaults to their "For You Page" (FYP), based on their proprietary algorithm, which is part of its "addictive" appeal.[1] They find themselves transfixed, scrolling through the default FYP, a distraction that was especially welcome during quarantine or lockdown due to the pandemic. The fact that the rationale behind the FYP curation is unknown to users—we don't know why the app suggests the videos it does, although we can determine (much of) the data it uses to determine the curation—means that the user experience of the app mirrors that of witchcraft, in that it's occult (hidden). The portmanteau for this phenomenon—technomancy—is itself a subculture of occult interest. Related to other forms of divination and occult practice (cartomancy, necromancy), technomancy

DOI: 10.4324/9781003280705-12

refers to the magical use of technology, whether to achieve a particular goal (that is, using technology to cast a spell or perform apparently supernatural acts) or to create a digital interface that is so unexpected and intense as an experience for users that the technology behind the effects is considered to be magic.[2]

Before the internet, knowledge about witchcraft was shared either in person or via specialized research, but since its early days, the internet has offered the tantalizing promise of finding and revealing secret knowledge. Not surprisingly, as public interest in witchcraft has skyrocketed in the twenty-first century, retailers and professional practitioners (who teach classes or offer readings, for example) have embraced the internet for making witchy products and services more widely available to the average American consumer.[3] On Instagram especially, accounts with witchy aesthetics attract followers who are also consumers of the products that either the creators themselves sell or are suggested and featured by these creators, some of whom are influencers. On Tumblr, Twitter, and YouTube, most witch-related content is informational or instructive, although many YouTubers will monetize their videos and provide affiliate (commission-earning) links in the description box. While several WitchTok creators also offer oc-cult services, generally speaking, the purpose of the witch subculture on this platform is both aesthetic and educational—a digital update to the oral tradition of sharing knowledge about witchcraft. Like other queer subcultures with which it frequently overlaps, WitchTok con-tributes to identity formation, allowing users to perform (and try on) their witchy selves.[4]

As "a cultural force that defines Gen Z," with half of TikTok's view-ership estimated to be in their mid-twenties or younger, it is not sur-prising that self-identified "baby witches" are the primary audience for the educational videos found on WitchTok.[5] Several of these lessons mirror cooking video lessons by sharing recipes while demonstrating methods for casting spells, but the call-and-response format of TikTok and its citational critique options also provide opportunities for pur-portedly more experienced witches to dispel or challenge rumors and myths about witchcraft. These last two categories of video—the stitch/ duet option that has been described as a kind of call-and-response conversation, and the citational critique format, in which creators re-contextualize lyrics or memes as a means of performed analysis— both fall into the category of adaptation dramaturgy, or *adapturgy*.[6] A vital part of collaborating to make theater, dramaturgy is the art of listening and asking questions about all stages of performance, from inception to reception by audiences.[7] As a dramaturg who specializes in adaptation, I appreciate WitchTok videos that foreground processes of adaptation: the call-and-response and the citational critique. In both cases, creators are taking a digital artifact (a meme, another Tik-Tok video, or a screen shot, for example) and adapting it based on research (of a wide and frustratingly opaque variety, most of it based in personal experience or popular culture), before offering it to the public as a new performance. Thus, although all of TikTok's offerings can be seen as performance adaptations, with varying levels of visible dramaturgy undergirding them, the duets/stitches and citational critiques are most transparently adaptations. As such, the tools of adapturgy can be used to unpack and better understand the subculture of these types of WitchTok videos, led by the guiding dramaturgical question for theatrical adaptations: *Why this lesson as WitchTok now?*[8] In what follows, I briefly outline the scope of these call-and-response and citational critique educational offerings within the WitchTok subculture, with this question guiding my review.

Magic Mirror

From its origins as a means of "remixing and repurposing music," TikTok has accumulated a staggering array of posts that continue to remix, often without a focus on music or dance.[9] Duets and stitches encourage "creators to capitalize on a sound's success to gain views while also providing opportunity for alternative interpretation," by featuring the post they remix either side-by-side with the creator's commentary (duets) or allowing them to insert snippets interspersed with their response (stitches).[10] On my FYP in August 2021 for example, many duets/stitches mirrored contentious and life-threatening debates in the wider American culture about the COVID-19 vaccine, masking mandates, and their efficacy or perceived danger. Because many of these are made by scientists, medical professionals, or other credentialed creators, responding to calls or posts made by largely non-credentialed creators, the responses are based in facts that can be verified like most other public claims. Within the WitchTok community, however, the basis for legitimacy is more slippery, especially when the calls and/or responses originate from a previously unknown account. Because there is no singular path for witchcraft (much less a universally shared text), specious-sounding claims may in fact have value when seen through the lens of a different system. More problematic still is the fact that by definition occult knowledge is meant to be hidden and that many (but not all) witches' rituals are part of a closed practice.

The recognition of closed practices itself has become a trend within WitchTok duets and stitches, typically featuring a response that calls out creators whose posts reveal their ignorance about cultural appropriation. White baby witches are reprimanded for appropriating aspects of Voodoo, Hoodoo, Brujería, or indigenous magic, as one might expect, since these practices involve not only initiation and apprenticeship, but carry culturally specific histories of calling upon supernatural forces as part of their larger resistance to white supremacy and colonizing violence. What is perhaps less expected is the debate over who should have access to witchcraft linked to faery magic and the use of tarot cards. These last two examples—the fae and tarot reading— are extremely popular within WitchTok, but apparently attempts have been made by white users of the platform to suggest that faeries only work with witches who have Celtic or Welsh ancestry, and that only those of Roma descent can practice divination using the tarot. But neither claim holds water, a point that WitchTok has taken up using the dialogue function of duets and stitches—one user who claims to be a "fairy folklorist," named Druid Emo Boy (@dust_hallow), for example, addressed these claims in a December 2020 post. While not a traditional duet or stitch, @dust_hallow begins his video by impersonating those who believe "the fae/good neighbors only exist on celtic lands you can't work with them in america [*sic*]," by teaching viewers that fairies (especially the Sídhe) are believed to be seafaring beings (with possible origins in what we now call India) who should never be considered landlocked.[11] Another user from Ireland (Teagan) notes the hypocrisy with which the primarily white viewership of TikTok treated the notion of closed practice, depending on who was gatekeeping whom. In her March 2021 post, @anirishpagan asks "Why were we [Celtic pagans] treated with reverence (for 'protecting' our culture) and why are POC practitioners still treated like dirt for wanting to do the exact same thing?"[12]

Questions about cultural appropriation for tarot card use are more complex, however. In March 2021, Esme (@weatherwax_80) stitched the claim (made by @skankx) that tarot is closed and that the cards are not for divination but "a way for Romani to connect with their ancestors," responding that, while Esme (who is Romani) understands the "well intentioned" attempt to guard tarot, "this is not the advocacy you think it is." Other commenters on @skankx's original claim pointed out the influence of the Kabbalah on tarot decks, going so far as to suggest that the claim was "really antisemitic."[13] While these snapshots of the debate hardly capture the breadth of conversation about practices being closed or open, they do highlight the racial and ethnic dimensions of TikTok's proprietary algorithm, by demonstrating the frequency of questionable gatekeeping by white creators on the platform compared to legitimate critiques made by creators from the global majority about white practitioners who co-opt closed practices.

While the open/closed practice debates are ongoing, there is another trending use of WitchTok's call-and-response potential that does not use the duets or stitch option: conversations between self-identified witches and the deities with whom they claim to work. Many of these posts use a filter option to entirely whiten (or blacken) the creator's eyes for the responses from the deities they perform, but otherwise enact both themselves as witches and their deities in casual dress, looking otherwise the way they typically look on their profiles. One of the most popular creators within WitchTok, Frankie Anne (@chaoticwitchaunt), has several deity conversation posts using this filter. In one post, Frankie begins to shuffle a deck of tarot cards, followed by a jump cut to Frankie using the "white pupils" filter, with a caption stating that this is Freyja, who promptly claims the tarot deck as her own, instructing Frankie to place the deck on their altar to Freyja, specifying that Frankie should "put it under my nice big amber chunk."[14] Frankie enacts both themselves Freyja in this video, with both characters' speech spoken aloud as well as captioned. The fact that creators who thrive in this subculture of witch practice online would enact (what they consider to be) the deities they worship and follow is itself remarkable, but however unexpected it is to view (and perhaps *because* it is startling to see casual performances of gods), staging the self-as-deity occurs throughout WitchTok.

This preference for deities over the Wiccan practice of worshipping a duo of a god and goddess to represent the pantheon suggests just how influential WitchTok is to the witch-curious members of Gen Z.[15] In previous generations, and certainly for my own Gen X folks, searches for American witchcraft educational materials defaulted to Wiccan practice, with rare exceptions.

The familiarity and casualness with which WitchTokers stage conversations with gods can be charming but it can also be taken to extremes: in August 2021, as US forces began to withdraw from Afghanistan, rumors spread about a group of Reddit-based witches attempting to bind or otherwise quell the Taliban's power. The notion that witches would conjure for political gain is itself not remarkable, but because some of these witches claimed to confront Allah directly, the anti-Taliban Redditors went viral. "You can't hex god—the fuck?!" was a typical response among experienced witches on several platforms, many of whom questioned whether the entire event was meant as a publicity stunt or elaborate spoof.[16] While the Reddit group where this originated has now become an extended joke, the larger phenomenon of new-to-witchcraft practitioners perceiving themselves as capable of "slaying" or otherwise being equal to deities continues unabated.[17]

Dramaturgically speaking, these trends point to a general desire among young adults to feel powerful and capable of using witchcraft to solve problems their elders cannot or will not resolve. From global warming to the "endless wars" to racial injustice and misogyny, the problems of the twenty-first century appear insurmountable without divine intervention.[18] As "digital natives," Zoomers primarily find community and research online, a trait that became exacerbated during US lockdowns due to the pandemic.[19] Their curated online selves, documented through "selfies" they post, encourage young adults to become adepts at seeing themselves differently through various filters—for Gen Z, transforming oneself digitally is commonplace. In witch parlance, what a filter achieves digitally is called *glamour*, an enchantment or manifestation spell that is cast by witches to change how they are seen.[20] Is it any wonder that this generation would flock to the WitchTok subculture, given the ways that social media have encouraged Zoomers to ask themselves "who is the fairest of them all?"[21]

Witch, Please

The "selfie" is a cornerstone of social media, but the practice of sharing (spoken and musical) sound is part of TikTok's appeal: it can be social, like sharing a trending dance or "get to know you" questionnaire, but it can also function as critique, either obliquely or directly. Whereas the duet/stitch option relies upon integrating and answering another creator's post, either partially or fully, what distinguishes the citational critique is its recontextualization, explanation, or deconstruction of sound and image. In the context of WitchTok, this category of videos typically includes reorienting a mundane or profane trend from popular culture within a witch-relevant milieu. For example, a June 29, 2021 post by Lexi (@lightwands), "tarot cards as lyrics from bo burnham's inside [*sic*]" begins with a shot of the creator holding a fanned-out deck of Tarot with the card details facing the camera, behind the title. The video then moves to several overhead shots of individual cards, while Burnham's lyrics play, accompanied by modified captioning: the first shot is of The Devil card, with the caption "f*ck their wives drink their blood," while the audio of this line (uncensored) is heard. We then see

11 tarot cards matched with lyrics from corresponding songs in the same manner.[22]

The effect of this offering is compelling—first, it builds on knowledge that TikTok viewership would almost certainly have: *Inside*, the Netflix special made by Burnham alone in the midst of the COVID-19 pandemic and released in May 2021 to widespread acclaim, especially among Zoomers. This one-man show resonated with audiences, as one of the first full-length performances to address the strange circumstances of 2020 with an unflinching vulnerability couched in dark comedy. Called a "musical fantasy about terrible realities" by NPR critic Linda Holmes, *Inside* "slam cuts between footage of [Burnham] sitting at a keyboard singing … and footage of himself in a near-catatonic state, as his hair and beard get longer and scragglier."[23] Given that the audience for TikTok itself grew exponentially during lockdowns imposed during 2020 due to the pandemic, the subject matter of *Inside* directly relates to the ennui felt by TikTok users and creators. Indeed, since its release, *Inside* sound bites have been frequently incorporated into the platform, establishing Burnham's lyrics and commentary within TikToker's lexicon.

Within the educational scope of WitchTok, relying upon *Inside* as a shared cultural reference allows creators to provide a mnemonic device for learning witchcraft. In the example cited above, Lexi (@lightwands) uses it as short-hand for Tarot card meanings—The Devil card, for example, signifies the "shadow side" of humanity, or "our internal struggles with external temptations, and the choices we have in the matter."[24] To link this card with a line from Burnham's "Bezos I" tracks for progressive-minded users who consider Jeff Bezos to exemplify the 1% of extremely wealthy Americans whose advantage over the working class grew exponentially during lockdown, as consumers relied upon Amazon for reliable delivery. The connection of The Sun card with the upbeat percussive lyrics from "Unpaid Intern" also tracks, as this "is a joyous card: good things are coming or have already arrived."[25] While the melody of "Unpaid Intern" suggests joy, the lyrics themselves stand in sharp contrast ("Barely people, somehow legal")—this irony is key to Burnham's appeal to Gen Z audiences, whose preference for bitter and self-deprecating humor was itself heightened during the isolation (and in many cases, return home from college) experienced in spring 2020 through summer 2021.

Comments made on Lexi's Burnham/Tarot citational critique affirm this familiarity and the effectiveness of the lesson: as @atarii_ states in the top comment, "this has taught me more than all of my guidebooks." Another user, @lunarlu adds, "I hate that this makes sense," a comment that is liked and responded to by @lightwands herself: "honestly me too a little." Other commenters take the idea and run with it, suggesting (for example) that "I feel like 'well, well, look who's inside again' would've been a PERFECT opportunity for the hermit" (@hihijinks).[26] And, in true TikTok fashion, other creators take inspiration from Lexi, posting their own take on the concept, many of whom use Lexi's mix of Burnham's lyrics verbatim, connecting them with Tarot cards of their choice. Sometimes, they choose the same cards, but other times, they modify Lexi's curation—one creator (@bystephkirsten) took the advice offered by @hihijinks above, matching The Hermit card to the lyrics about being inside again from "Goodbye," rather than the Four of Swords that Lexi chose.[27] Another user (@rosebirdwitch), also citing Lexi and using her mash-up of Burnham's lyrics, assigned The Hermit card to "there it is again, that funny feeling" ("Welcome to the Internet").[28] The variety here is especially useful for those learning the Tarot, as it reinforces one of the most challenging aspects of the deck: the cards themselves may have canonical readings that students can learn from guidebooks, but in practical usage, the interpretation of any single card is never made in isolation. Like all divination methods, practitioners of Tarot are expected to read the cards in context. Depending on the situation, that context could be a question asked, or the role a particular card plays in relationship to other cards drawn (and when/how, based on the "spread," if multiple cards are pulled), but it also always relies on what the Tarot user's intuition or clairvoyance suggests.

TikTok encourages such heterogenous multiplicity throughout the platform, but within the WitchTok subculture, it is particularly significant that the method mirrors the content. When exploring witchcraft, baby witches usually conduct their research alone, through a combination of online resources and publications. Whether seekers are still "in the broom closet" or not, unless they have close friends or family members who identify as witches, within monotheistic cultures, there is likely an element of shame or a thrill of danger associated with their curiosity about witchcraft, making it more likely that they seek answers in solitude. With WitchTok, not only do they have a thriving online community of other baby (and elder) witches, but they are also constantly reminded that the "lack of dogmatism" central to occultism means that witches must always resist what William James (and Margot Adler) recognize as "contentment with the finite."[29] Far from finite, TikTok is notorious for its seemingly endless feed of videos offered on the default FYP, a feature that itself has been framed as a kind of magical spell to entrance users, allowing them to lose track of time and distract themselves from their surroundings.[30] To return to the question posed at the beginning of this essay, then, it appears that spells can certainly be taught digitally, but by whom (or what)? And to what end?

The meta-magic of WitchTok has not gone unnoticed: as one creator (@aspiring_alchemist) noted, "the same way TikTok and YouTube and all these platforms have an algorithm that can detect the kind of content they think you'd like…, the universe has an algorithm for you as well, and it's pretty much the exact same thing."[31] He goes on to suggest that this larger, cosmic algorithm responds based on where we put our energies, but it is "indifferent to what it serves you." In the same vein as technomancy (or any other divination tool), though, he reassures viewers that we still have control over our destiny: we can "train the algorithm" by directing our attention and engagement (with digital media as well as face-to-face interactions) according to our true preferences.[32] And those preferences appear to skew toward learning about witchcraft for a significant portion of TikTok's users, with 22 billion views (as of this writing) for the WitchTok hashtag alone, many of which originate from self-identified baby witches. May they wield their power—in both the material and the metaphysical world—wisely.

Notes

1 Regarding the addictive nature of TikTok and the way usage curates the FYP, see Melissa Blanco Borelli and Madison Moore [*sic*], "TikTok, Friendship, and Sipping Tea, or How to Endure a Pandemic," *The International Journal of Screendance* 12 (2021), accessed September 17, 2021, https://screendancejournal.org/article/view/8238/6120.

2 Joshua Madara, "What Is Technomancy?" *Technomancy 101: Advanced Cybermagic for Beginners* (2018), accessed September 5, 2021, https://technomancy101.com/technomancy/.

3 As one example of how contemporary witches monetize their internet presence, Chaotic Witch Aunt has platforms on TikTok, Instagram, and YouTube, as well as a website that sells "merch," referring not to material items in this case but to various interactive Tarot readings they offer, ranging from "3 card reading" (20 USD) to "Deity Identification Reading" (60 USD), accessed September 22, 2021, https://chaoticwitchaunt.com.

4 Luis Loya and Elaine Almeida, "Things that shouldn't have Gay Energy but Do Anyways: CTI, Remixes and TikTok Duets." *Flow*, September 29, 2020, accessed September 22, 2021 https://www.flowjournal.org/2020/09/cti-remixes-tiktok-duets/.

5 Trevor Boffone, *Renegades: Digital Dance Cultures from Dubsmash to TikTok* (Oxford: Oxford University Press, 2021), 27.

6 Jane Barnette, *Adapturgy: The Dramaturg's Art and Theatrical Adaptation* (Carbondale: Southern Illinois University Press, 2017).

7 For more about the capacious art of dramaturgy, see Michael Mark Chemers, *Ghost Light: An Introductory Handbook for Dramaturgy* (Carbondale: Southern Illinois University Press, 2010) and Magda Romanska, editor, *The Routledge Companion to Dramaturgy* (London: Routledge, 2015).
8 The question for theatrical adaptations is "Why This Source as Theatre Now?" See Barnette, *Adapturgy*: 36.
9 Ethan Bresnick, "Intensified Play: Cinematic Study of TikTok Mobile App," *ResearchGate*, April 2019, accessed September 22, 2021, https://www.researchgate.net/publication/335570557_Intensified_Play_Cinematic_study_of_TikTok_mobile_app: 6.
10 Loya and Almeida, "Gay Energy."
11 @dust_hallow, December 7, 2020. TikTok.
12 @anirishpagan, "Either Keep the Energy for POC or Fuck Right Off," March 11, 2021. TikTok.
13 Comment by @continuousd3ath, March 11, 2021, on @skankx post of the same date. TikTok.
14 @chaoticwitchaunt, "Who Wants to See the Tarot Deck That Freyja Has Literally CLAIMED as Hers," March 17, 2021. TikTok.
15 "Wicca," March 23, 2018, *History.com*, accessed September 7, 2021, https://www.history.com/topics/religion/wicca. The popularity of deity worship can also be traced to other online communities like Tumblr, Instagram, and Pinterest.
16 @afro_spiritual, "Most Ridiculous Thing I've Heard since Hexing the fae or the moon…," August 20, 2021. TikTok.
17 This reference to "slaying" comes from one of the Reddit posts from the anti-Taliban hexing attempts, where the user's final sentence reads, "Allah is much stronger than I first imagined and we will have to do this together if we want to slay a god." From @dumbest_bitch, posted August 19, 2021 in "Bewitch the Taliban" on Reddit.
18 The term "endless war" has been used to describe several different conflicts, but in a US contemporary context, typically refers to the war on terrorism waged primarily in the Middle East. For more on this concept, see "Endless War: A Term with a History and Definition," *New America*, accessed September 7, 2021, https://www.newamerica.org/international-security/reports/defining-endless-wars/endless-war-a-term-with-a-history-and-a-definition/.
19 Anthony Turner, "Generation Z: Technology and Social Interest," *The Journal of Individual Psychology* 71, no. 2 (2015):103–113, 104.
20 As Pam Grossman notes, "The words 'glamour' and 'grimoire' and 'grammar' all come from the same root, so you can really see this idea of creativity and magic being interlinked." Jenni Miller, "Meet Pam Grossman, the Terry Gross of Witches." *Vulture*, June 4, 2019, accessed September 7, 2021, https://www.vulture.com/2019/06/pam-grossman-witch-interview.html.
21 The quotation from *Snow White and the Seven Dwarves* (1937) is often misremembered as "Mirror, mirror on the wall…" when in fact it begins, "Magic mirror on the wall." Janaki Jitchotvisut, "10 Popular Movie Quotes You've Probably Been Saying Wrong All Along," *Insider*, November 28, 2018, accessed September 7, 2021, https://www.insider.com/movie-quotes-youre-getting-wrong-2018-11.

22 @lightwands, "Tarot Cards as Lyrics from Bo Burnham's Inside," June 29, 2021. TikTok. These lyrics come from (in order of appearance) "Bezos I," "Shit," "Welcome to the Internet," "That Funny Feeling," "Content," "Content" (again), "Don't Wanna Know," "Sexting," "Unpaid Intern," "Bezos I," "Goodbye," and "All Time Low," all songs from Bo Burnham, *Inside (The Songs)*, Republic Records (June 2021).

23 Linda Holmes, "Bo Burnham's 'Inside' is a Musical Fantasy about Terrible Realities," *NPR*, June 4, 2021, accessed September 7, 2021. https://www.npr.org/2021/06/04/1002491153/bo-burnhams-inside-is-a-musical-fantasy-about-terrible-realities.

24 Rachel True, *True Heart Intuitive Tarot Guidebook* (Boston, MA: Houghton Mifflin Harcourt, 2020), "The Devil," 117.

25 Ibid., "The Sun," 137.

26 @lightwands, comments on "Tarot Cards as Lyrics from Bo Burnham's Inside," June 29, 2021. TikTok.

27 @bystephkirsten, "The Tarot as Lyrics from Bo Burnham's 'Inside'," July 14, 2021. TikTok.

28 @rosebirdwitch, "Major Arcana Tarot Cards as Lyrics from Bo Burnham's Inside," June 30, 2021. TikTok.

29 Margot Adler, *Drawing Down the Moon: Witches, Druids, Goddess-Worshippers, and Other Pagans in America*, Completely Revised and Updated (New York: Penguin, 2006), 12.

30 The FYP has been called "one of the most addictive scrolling experiences on the Internet." Jing Zeng, Crystal Abidin, and Mike S. Schäfer, "Research Perspectives on TikTok and Its Legacy Apps," *International Journal of Communication* 15 (2021): 3161–3172, 3163.

31 @aspiring_alchemist, "THE UNIVERSE HAS AN ALGORITHM!!" September 1, 2021. TikTok.

32 Ibid.

9 Wellness TikTok

Morning Routines, Eating Well, and Getting Ready to Be "That Girl"

Katlin Marisol Sweeney-Romero

In April 2021, the TikTok trend now known as "#ThatGirl" began to dominate the subcultures of the app focused on beauty, lifestyle, study habits, and healthy eating. Videos uploaded to the platform that feature this hashtag—usually with at least one other hashtag such as #Self-careTikTok, #HealthyLifestyle, #MorningRoutine, #DailyBlog or #MiniBlog, #Motivation, #Productivity, or #Aesthetic—foreground the habits that "high-achieving" women in their 20s and 30s suggest are foundational to their personal and professional success. Content creators who embrace the #ThatGirl aesthetic effectively produce video collages devoted to the pursuit of a systematic lifestyle before, during, and after the 9-5 workday or school day. By editing together various one-second and five-second video clips of their daily activities and combining them with self-reflections and "mood" appropriate music, these creators develop step-by-step templates for "wellness" that their viewers are encouraged to adopt to start their respective wellness journey.

Consistent across these videos is the creator's emphasis that achieving wellness occurs through carefully assembling and following a manicured morning routine that gradually translates to "becoming that girl." As writers for the popular press have observed, these videos are structured as mini vlogs of daily routines that follow a formula: wake up as early as 5 a.m.; put on a "matching set" of workout clothes to go to the gym or work out from home; prepare a colorful but modest, healthy breakfast; hydrate with lemon water while also drinking a matcha; apply name brand body-care products in the shower and hang eucalyptus leaves from the showerhead; follow a skincare regimen comprised of products with minimalist packaging and ingredients; change into a matching "lounge set" or color-coordinated work attire; light a candle while writing in a copy of *The Five-Minute Journal*; and

DOI: 10.4324/9781003280705-13

grab a "treat" at a coffee shop while walking or driving to a corporate job or university class.[1]

Morning routine videos are filmed in bright lighting, are enhanced by a sunrise, and typically feature cohesive, "neutral" tones such as all-white or grey bedding, workout clothes, and room décor. Some TikTok profiles supplement these hyper-productive morning routines with soothing nighttime routines at either the end of a daily vlog (e.g., a "day to night" vlog), or upload them as stand-alone posts (e.g., nighttime routines). In contrast to the morning routine, nighttime routine videos are dimly lit by bedroom string lights, often include a sunset, and show creators running a bath, watching a movie, reading a book, making dinner, or lighting name brand candles or incense after getting home from work. The wellness pursued by #ThatGirl is ultimately designed to uphold productivity as an idealized form of empowerment, evidenced by how morning routine posts outnumber nighttime routines posted under the hashtag, and by how content creators perform rest in their content rather than actually resting (i.e., turning off their phone and disconnecting from social media).

This chapter considers how the #ThatGirl trend on TikTok derives its influence in part by converging elements from the beauty, lifestyle, study habit, and healthy eating subgenres on the platform, which culminates in the creation of a multifaceted Wellness TikTok subculture. By incorporating self-improvement strategies from each of these subgenres into their online self-production, content creators who post #ThatGirl videos generate and endorse an informal, multistep "wellness plan" that facilitates the average woman's transformation into her optimal self at home and at work. These videos imply that the morning routine is a universal formula for success that can be customized to suit any woman's lifestyle so long as she puts in the effort necessary to achieve her goals. However, this essay argues that the aspirational lifestyle of habit-tracking, healthy eating, and self-care mediated through #ThatGirl videos on TikTok ascribes to white supremacist views of beauty and productivity by idealizing the "look" of wellness as that of a woman who is laboring at all times—for her job and for her body—and who is young, white or white-passing, thin, able-bodied, cisgender, and whose gender performance abides by heteronormative expectations of femininity. Through brief textual analysis of how motivational speeches, attention to time, and "productive" habits play "on a loop" in these videos, this chapter demonstrates how the #ThatGirl trend contributes to mainstream beauty pressures by instructing girls and women to perceive of time off as an opportunity to optimize rather than rest.

Idealized Internet Girlhoods: From YouTuber Self-brands to Going Viral on TikTok

The aspirational, daily vlog format of Wellness TikTok takes cues from the videos produced by beauty and wellness "gurus" in the beauty, lifestyle, and wellness communities on YouTube in the late 2000s, all of which contributed to the social media influencer boom on Instagram in the 2010s that preceded TikTok's gradual surge in popularity in the United States starting in 2018. In their "how-to" instructional videos and "a day in the life" vlogs, content creators known as "YouTubers" instruct their viewers on requested topics such as creating a makeup look, developing a personal style, decorating their home, shopping on a budget, improving their performance at work, and preparing meals. As celebrity studies scholars have argued in their analyses of social media influencers as micro-celebrity practitioners, YouTubers and Instagram influencers invest time in creating an online self or public persona that initially mimics elements of traditional celebrity branding before proceeding to develop new, original forms of self-presentation on the Internet.[2] The popularity of these creators and the longevity of their careers are predicated on what media and girlhood studies scholar Emma Maguire describes as the perceived authenticity of the YouTuber's "automedial self," or the self-representations they put forth in their videos and supplement with other online activity like tweets and blog posts that circulate through social media over time.[3] To initiate and sustain audience engagement with their content in the form of likes and comments on posts, video shares, channel subscriptions, and profile "follows," YouTubers and Instagram influencers refine what media and girlhood studies scholar Sarah Banet-Weiser terms "the post-feminist self-brand": a process by which the girl creator purportedly achieves a sense of empowerment as she "authorizes herself to be consumed through her own self-production" of an identity through online spaces like YouTube.[4] In keeping with Maguire and Banet-Weiser, what becomes clear is how the self-brand makes publicly visible the girl self and commodifies her into a product that can be "branded, managed, and distributed within a cultural marketplace,"[5] which consumers gain access to through their own automedial selves on platforms like Instagram or Facebook.[6]

The development of a self-brand, which remains conducive to achieving "Instafame" through YouTube and Instagram, however, does not translate to TikTok due to the app's trend-based design. Social media studies scholar Crystal Abidin argues that TikTokers are often not curating a persona as a requisite for engagement, "but instead are actively and very quickly adapting from the latest trends and viral practices on TikTok, to attempt varieties of styles—across hashtags, keywords, filters, audio memes, narrative memes—to aim for the For You Page, or the 'golden ticket' that would allow one to gain an immense number of followers overnight."[7] That is, TikTokers can reallocate the time typically spent by content creators on self-brand curation to focus instead on the creative labor of incorporating trending sounds, dances, terms, and aesthetics into the videos they produce as often as possible to increase the chances that their videos are seen by the public. Media scholar Andrea Ruehlicke emphasizes the significance of TikTok's trend-based design in that "the app drops the user into an always playing stream" of content on the "For You Page" (also known as the "FYP"), which limits user-direction beyond liking a video, following a creator, or swiping past the video if uninterested or done watching.[8] According to Ruehlicke, "belonging" to a community on TikTok differs from other social media platforms in that the user must consciously devote time to engaging with videos—that is, providing the algorithm with enough user data—and "demonstrate the correct interests to be read as belonging to a variety of TikTok spaces."[9] Without doing so, what is considered more "niche" content is unlikely to appear on a user's For You Page unless it is already trending and automatically moved to this page. Social media scholars Aparajita Bhandari and Sara Bimo argue that this design makes TikTok unique in that it creates an "algorithmized self" of "intra rather than interpersonal connection," based on its trending algorithm, which is advertised as custom to each profile, and the individual's respective content creation on the platform. By contrast, other forms of social media give way to a "networked self" in which an online self is generated through engagement with their social circle (i.e., Instagram followers or Facebook friends).[10]

Although TikTok as a platform has effectively generated the potential of social media stardom through viral trends and challenges rather than self-brands, the platform functions as what theater and performance studies scholar Trevor Boffone terms a "white space" that has given way to "The D'Amelio Effect." As he writes elsewhere and in Chapter 1 of this collection, "The D'Amelio Effect" recognizes how white TikTokers, particularly white teenage girls like Charli D'Amelio or young white women like Addison Rae, rise to prominence on the platform by copying, appropriating, and profiting from the creative labor of Black teenage girls, who by contrast receive little to no credit for their work.[11] After dancing the #RenegadeChallenge that was choreographed and created by Jalaiah Harmon, D'Amelio's career skyrocketed from social media fame to legacy media opportunities like reality television and a Super Bowl commercial. The mainstream success of D'Amelio exemplifies how, according to Boffone, TikTok as a platform "promotes whiteness while obfuscating Blackness and the cultural contributions of the Black artists who sing these songs and the Black dancers who choreograph the corresponding dance challenges."[12] Similarly, media and girlhood studies scholar Melanie Kennedy argues that Charli D'Amelio's dominance as the most-followed TikToker is reflective of how "algorithmic suppression and spectacularisation render some girlhoods hypervisible and others hidden in the shadows."[13] More specifically, she contends that D'Amelio's meteoric rise on the platform is a "continuation" of how normative girlhood is foregrounded in celebrity culture, and how the cultural site of the girl's bedroom contributes to the "spectacular mundanity" that renders girls like D'Amelio "goofy and relatable" to their audience.

That is, while white girl and women TikTokers can achieve popularity by appropriating and performing to Black creators' original sounds, dances, and aesthetics, Black girl and women TikTokers as trend-making cultural producers remain undervalued despite their contributions. The viral hashtag #BamaRushTok, which dominated the platform in August 2021 and followed young women as they rushed sororities at the University of Alabama, also reinforces this trend. Among the most popular videos uploaded with this hashtag were #ootd, or Outfit of the Day, during which one or more aspiring sorority sisters would model an itemized breakdown of what she was wearing and where she had purchased it. Among the many white women contributing content to #BamaRush was a single, mixed-race woman named Makayla Culpepper (@whatwouldjimmybuffettdo) whose #ootd videos for rush made her the undeniable "star" of the hashtag. Both her mediated personality and presence as a non-white girl in the #BamaRush space were celebrated by viewers who commented on these posts that Culpepper was "the most real" of any of the girls posting about rush. However, she was unexpectedly dropped from sororities over a video of her underage drinking, which prompted many users to question if Culpepper's mixed-race identity and heightened popularity compared to white women on #BamaRushTok was the actual reason for her dismissal.[14] That is, even when Black creators temporarily experience visibility or popularity in viral TikTok hashtags, platform-based or external intervention make it notably more difficult for a Black creator or creator of color to sustain career longevity and "earn" mainstream support that white creators often automatically receive.

Becoming "That Girl" by Example: Self-motivation, Habit-tracking, and Scheduled Time

The viral #ThatGirl trend, which has more than 1.3 billion views, is Wellness TikTok's most recognizable trending hashtag, and through its reverence for a white, cis-hetero-patriarchal beauty ideal that envisions a route to empowerment through optimizing one's productivity at home and at work, exemplifies what Boffone characterizes as how "TikTok is designed to uphold whiteness as not just the norm, but as something aspirational."[15] While the "The D'Amelio Effect" is on full-display as white girl and women creators rise to prominence through appropriating Black creators' cultural production under viral hashtags such as #RenegadeChallenge and #BamaRushTok, the #ThatGirl trend dominates Wellness TikTok as another subset of "relatable" girlhood, one that also relies on the bedroom as a cultural site of identity construction and online public performance. More so than these other spaces, however, the #ThatGirl trend explicitly foregrounds the home in the creator's content as the site that makes tangible her systematic approach to perfection (i.e., spaces where she can project her fitness videos on the wall, lay out her yoga mat, and prepare her meals), and in doing so, idealizes thin, white girls and women as a universally desirable beauty ideal that all should aspire toward.

The pursuit of an aspirational #ThatGirl look and lifestyle through an organized series of routines framed as "self-care" resembles the self-brand logic that propelled beauty and wellness gurus and Instagram influencers to the forefront of social media from the late 2000s onward, even as TikTok as a platform has strayed from this formula for success. As girl and women creators film their morning routines from their bedroom and suggest home décor/organization to be a contributor to their success, they develop credibility as a wellness cultural producer by using recognizable elements from YouTube and Instagram such as makeup and skincare collections, color-coded wardrobes, and perfectly organized kitchens to facilitate their wellness journeys. Importantly, media scholar Florencia García-Rapp details at-length in her study of beauty YouTuber Bubzbeauty how online communities like beauty YouTube are comprised of both a commercial sphere featuring "content-oriented videos and market-oriented videos" such as tutorials and product reviews, as well as a community sphere consisting of "relational and motivational" videos such as vlogs and self-help guides.[16] Creators on Wellness TikTok merge elements of the commercial and community spheres through the #ThatGirl trend by producing videos in which they edit together a series of brief video clips that document each step of their morning routine, overlay them with either written or spoken motivations in first- or second-person address, and include background music that matches the pacing of the edit.

In some videos, the motivation is concise and delivered through the post description, as in the case of a video uploaded by @virgohabits on May 27, 2021, which features the caption "new day, new opportunity #5amclub #MorningRoutine #Productivity #ThatGirl ib: @vanessatiiu." The video itself is more detailed, as it is visually bookended by a MacBook laptop showing the start time of 5:30 a.m. and the end time of 8:00 a.m. as the video cycles through clips "on a loop" of the creator getting out of bed and looking in a floor-length mirror, journaling, working out, changing clothes, preparing breakfast, and starting her work for the day. These video clips are supplemented by brief, written descriptions on each part of the content creator's morning routine, which are overlayed on the related video clip to produce a series of instructions that read, "THAT girl morning routine," "wake up early," "make bed," "workout set," "journal + plan," "yoga + pilates," "lounge set," "healthy breakfast," "work + study."

Similarly, in a video uploaded by @wellnesswithshreya on October 5, 2021, the caption "Morning routines that get me excited for my 9–5s #MorningRoutine, #ThatGirl, #wfh, #Motivation, #Productivity" is displayed beneath a video set to an excerpt from the *Gossip Girl* theme as clips of her morning routine play on-screen. While this vlog does not include small details such as written descriptions overlayed on each video clip, it demonstrates a more casual approach to #ThatGirl by visualizing how some creators rely on video clips of journaling, grabbing coffee before work, and making their bed to convey their daily commitment to balance and wellness. In other videos, the motivation is delivered through audio, as in the case of a video uploaded by @annasjournal on September 27, 2021, but similarly relies on video clips to show by example how to practice a wellness routine. The video opens with text that reads "productive morning routine" and features hashtags that include #MondayMotivation, #MorningRoutine, and #HealthyLifestyle. It features an audio clip set to instrumental music of lifestyle YouTuber Emma Chamberlain stating, "The second that you stop getting in your own way, and you're kind to yourself, and you're graceful with yourself, it's crazy to see how you blossom." As the audio plays, the content creator is shown waking up, changing into workout clothes, following the "Trainingsplan" organized on her MacBook laptop, showering, making breakfast, making coffee, and sitting down to eat.

In mini vlogs like these and others uploaded with #ThatGirl tagged, the comment sections feature other users posting compliments about the creator's appearance, requesting more information on where to purchase items shown in the video, and asking for recommendations on how to get started on their own wellness journey. These comment sections reflect how it is through the content creator's embodiment of the #ThatGirl aesthetic, and the repetitive, normalized framing of thin white bodies as the optimal beauty ideal to aspire toward, that other girls and women are compelled to participate in the trend of producing and regulating their wellness. What remains insidious about this version of relatable girlhood, however, is the suggestion that the only obstacle to achieving the aesthetic is the user's lack of dedication or effort toward curating the diet, exercise plan, wardrobe, and schedule necessary to become #ThatGirl in her own right. That is, rather than problematize or disrupt how whiteness and thin bodies are codified as perfect symbols of wellness in diet culture and mainstream media, the #ThatGirl trend reinforces it by generating a social pressure for all girls and women to perceive of their online self as incomplete without adhering to this aesthetic.

Notes

1 See Sahar Arshad, "What Does It Mean to Be 'That Girl'?" *Bustle*, August 11, 2021, https://www.bustle.com/life/what-does-that-girl-mean-tiktok-viral-trend; Michelle Santiago Cortés, "Who Is 'That Girl'? She's All of Us", *Refinery* 29, July 30, 2021, https://www.refinery29.com/en-gb/2021/07/10606927/that-girl-tiktok-gen-z-trend; Emma Gillman, "'That Girl' Is Everywhere Right Now. Here's Why I Find Her Toxic.'," *Mama Mia*, October 7, 2021, https://www.mamamia.com.au/that-girl-tiktok-trend/; Shamani Joshi, "I Tried to Be TikTok's 'That Girl' for a Week," *Vice*, September 9, 2021, https://www.vice.com/en/article/5db8ek/tiktok-youtube-viral-trend-that-girl-internet-genz-challenge; Ruchira Sharma, "Who Is 'That Girl' & Why Is TikTok Obsessed with Her?" *Refinery* 29, July 10, 2021, https://www.refinery29.com/en-gb/2021/07/10551994/tiktok-obsession-with-that-girl; Heather Wake, "Romanticizing? Or False Advertising? What's Really behind TikTok's 'That Girl' Trend," *Upworthy*, October 5, 2021, https://www.upworthy.com/tiktok--that-girl-trends, and Hannah Yasharoff, "What TikTok's Viral 'That Girl' Trend Isn't Showing You – and Why That Matters," *USA Today*, October 1, 2021, https://news.yahoo.com/tiktoks-viral-girl-trend-isnt-120042853.html.
2 See Alison Hearn and Stephanie Schoenhoff, "From Celebrity to Influencer: Tracing the Diffusion of Celebrity Value across the Data Stream," in *A Companion to Celebrity*, eds. P. David Marshall and Sean Redmond (Chichester, West Sussex: John Wiley & Sons, Inc, 2016), 194–212; Susie Khamis, Lawrence Ang, and Raymond Welling, "Self-Branding, 'Micro-Celebrity' and the Rise of Social Media Influencers," *Celebrity Studies* 8, no. 2 (2016): 191–208; P. David Marshall, "The Promotion and Presentation of the Self: Celebrity as Marker of Presentational Media," *Celebrity*

Studies 1, no. 1 (2010): 35–48; Alice E. Marwick, "You May Know Me from YouTube: (Micro-)Celebrity in Social Media," in *A Companion to Celebrity*, eds. P. David Marshall and Sean Redmond (Chichester, West Sussex: John Wiley & Sons, Inc, 2016), 334–350, and Bethany Usher, "Rethinking Microcelebrity: Key Points in Practice, Performance and Purpose," *Celebrity Studies* 11, no. 2 (2020): 171–188.

3 Emma Maguire, "Self-Branding, Hotness, and Girlhood in the Video Blogs of Jenna Marbles," *Biography* 38, no. 1, (2015), 73–75.

4 Sarah Banet-Weiser, "Branding the Post-Feminist Self: Girls' Video Production and YouTube," in *Mediated Girlhoods: New Explorations of Girls' Media Culture*, ed. Mary Celeste Kearney (New York: Peter Lang Publishing Inc, 2011), 277–294.

5 Ibid., 286.

6 Maguire, "Self-Branding, Hotness, and Girlhood in the Video Blogs of Jenna Marbles," 75.

7 Crystal Abidin, "Mapping Internet Celebrity on TikTok: Exploring Attention Economies and Visibility Labours," *Cultural Science Journal* 12, no. 1 (2021): 80.

8 Andrea Ruehlicke, "All the Content, Just for You: TikTok and Personalization," *Flow: A Critical Forum on Media and Culture* 27, no. 1 (2020), https://www.flowjournal.org/2020/10/content-just-for-you/.

9 Ibid.

10 Aparajita Bhandari and Sara Bimo, "TikTok and the 'Algorithmized Self': A New Model of Online Interaction," *AoIR Selected Papers of Internet Research* (2020): 1–3. https://journals.uic.edu/ojs/index.php/spir/issue/view/679; https://journals.uic.edu/ojs/index.php/spir/article/view/11172/9856

11 Trevor Boffone, *Renegades: Digital Dance Cultures from Dubsmash to TikTok* (New York: Oxford University Press, 2021), 2.

12 Trevor Boffone, "The D'Amelio Effect: TikTok, Charli D'Amelio, and the Construction of Whiteness," in *TikTok Cultures in the United States*, ed. Trevor Boffone (New York: Routledge, 2022), 7. See also Boffone, *Renegades*.

13 Melanie Kennedy. "'If the rise of the TikTok dance and e-girl aesthetic has taught us anything, it's that teenage girls rule the internet right now': TikTok Celebrity, Girls and the Coronavirus Crisis," *European Journal of Cultural Studies* 23, no. 6 (2020): 1073.

14 Dante Silva, "#BamaRushTok Has Taken Over," *Paper*, August 18, 2021, https://www.papermag.com/alabama-rush-tiktok-2654710069.html?rebelltitem=14#rebelltitem14.

15 Trevor Boffone, "The D'Amelio Effect: TikTok, Charli D'Amelio, and the Construction of Whiteness," in *TikTok Cultures in the United States*, ed. Trevor Boffone (New York: Routledge, 2022), 22.

16 Florencia García-Rapp, "Popularity markers on YouTube's Attention Economy: The Case of Bubzbeauty," *Celebrity Studies* 8, no. 2 (2017): 236.

10 Hype It Up
US Latinx Theater on TikTok

Elena Machado Sáez

Before and during the coronavirus pandemic, US Latinx theaters have struggled to build community recognition and support. TikTok offers such grassroots institutions the opportunity to expand their audience base as well as serving as a network for producing and circulating new cultural production. At the same time, US Latinx individuals use Tik-Tok to share their experiences as US Latinx performers on the mainstream stage, whether promoting their shows or critiquing racism. The exception to this rule is @genuinelygabriel who builds awareness about the existence of US Latinx playwrights, drawing attention to the lack of representation in theater curriculums. Overlap between institution building and these individual narratives is rare, which speaks to the potential and limits of these strategies on TikTok. Considering how US Latinx community-based and individual efforts occur in isolation, this chapter questions how TikTok's platform and aesthetics serve as tools for promoting US Latinx theatrical production. DIY Latinx theater traditions in a digital realm seek to build community, educate audiences, and engage in Latinx art-making. However, when observing the number of followers on these accounts and posts, it is clear that the work of this very chapter must be to amplify the work of such US Latinx institutions and individuals. Some of the theaters discussed include Teatro Audaz of San Antonio, Teatro Bravo in Phoenix, Borderlands Theater of Tucson, Teatro 8 of Miami, and Quemoción Production Company. I also spotlight the unique activist work of @genuinelygabriel and his series, "diverse shows you didn't learn about in your theater program!"

Emerging: US Latinx Theaters

The presence of US Latinx theater on TikTok is still emerging, as evidenced by the limited content dedicated to hashtags like #LatinxPlaywright, #LatinxActor, #LatinxDirector, #LatinaDirector, or

DOI: 10.4324/9781003280705-14

#LatinxTheater. Switching Latinx with Latine, Latina, or Latino does not serve to cast a wider net. No hashtags have yet been generated for AfroLatinx, Chicano, Nuyorican, Puerto Rican theater or playwrights. If one adds "plays" to any of these descriptors, the term is used as a verb rather than a noun, so the posts do not connect with US Latinx theater. Similarly, the word "drama" does not reference a literary genre, but rather a psychological experience or state of being. The only contributor to #DiversePlays and #LatinxPlays is @genuinelygabriel, which reveals that they are the originator of the hashtag itself. I will address Gabriel Rodriguez's work via @genuinelygabriel in greater detail later in this chapter, but this mention serves to highlight how the work of building the visibility of US Latinx theater is at a nascent stage. None of the above hashtags can be described as trending and the general use of hashtags by US Latinx theater institutions remains uneven. TikTok's prevailing dynamic of an individual talking to the camera means that such collective projects are at a disadvantage. The lack of resources, and at times social media savvy, leads US Latinx theaters to develop alternative ways of translating their work online. Nevertheless, a few are producing new work uniquely geared toward the TikTok platform.

Teatro Audaz, Teatro Bravo, Borderlands Theater, Teatro 8, and Quemoción Production Company are some of the most active US Latinx theater organizations on TikTok and their models for social media engagement are emblematic of broader trends. At the same time, their footprint in the TikTok landscape is hardly visible. Teatro 8 and Teatro Bravo exclusively use TikTok to advertise their shows, performance spaces, and share scenes from live shows. However, their marketing efforts do not seem to be productive. For example, Teatro 8 has 58 followers and 432 likes, while Teatro Bravo has 84 followers and 216 likes. The inability to build a broader base of TikTok followers does not appear to be a product of how theater organizations use the forum. Indeed, some of the most original work on TikTok by US Latinx theaters garners a similar level of attention and, by extension, investment.

By way of example, Teatro Audaz started their TikTok account as a way of relaunching their season after the pandemic closure, posting a series of videos starting on April 16, 2021 that highlighted the upcoming performance of Guillermo Reyes's *Men on the Verge of a His-panic Breakdown*. The videos promoted the play but also offered introductions to the individual actors (such as "Shining Star Jai Gonzalez") and short performances of dialogue from the script. The videos also provide a historiography of shows prior to the creation of the TikTok account, listing US Latinx plays such as *(Un)documents* by

Jesús I. Valles, *Curanderas and Chocolate* by Patricia Zamora, *Casa de Muñeca* by Liz Coronado Castillo, *Real Women Have Curves* by Josefina López, *Confessions of a Mexpatriate* by Raul Garza, and *Dos Chicanos, One Camino* by Gabriel Itzcoatl Luera. As a gesture of gratitude, another video showcases the board of Teatro Audaz, an important acknowledgment for a non-profit theater. Despite being such an active presence on TikTok, producing new content and promoting US Latinx-authored shows, Teatro Audaz only has 51 followers and 315 likes as of October 16, 2021.

Quemoción Production Company uses similar strategies with an even more expansive collection of posts and a strategic use of TikTok's hashtag promotions. Posts include original content that spotlights US Latinx artists and playwrights talking about their inspiration and views on the intersection of art and activism, for example, Henry Dominguez[1] and Yazmin Hernández.[2] Additionally, in-depth features of shows are used for promotion, for example, advertising shows like *Selena* and *Julia de Burgos* with video series of actors sharing their interpretation of these US Latinx historical figures and cultural icons. Taking advantage of trending hashtags that can highlight the organization's work, Quemoción Production Company contributed original material to the #SelenaChallenge and #HeightsChallenge. Beyond stage performances, their TikTok account amplifies the voices of US Latinx artists and educators as a way of boosting representation and supporting US Latinx culture. Take for instance the #quesazón "Coquito" series featuring @geeves_maldon's recipe for a Puerto Rican Christmas holiday drink and the "mikedrop" Cafecito series with commentary by @weauxisme and @ildamason. Garnering 2,424 likes for their account, Quemoción Production Company numbers of 67 followers do not do justice to their innovative strategies on TikTok.

Borderlands Theater has a limited presence on TikTok, but their broader approach to social media promotions warrants critical attention. Their TikTok posts are selections of videos from the "Digital Desmadre" project, which is explicitly aimed at young adults and encourages them to actively contribute to the work of the theater by producing new material for social media distribution. The call for participants was the following:

> Are you part of the New Generation full of ideas, parodies, and pop culture satire skits waiting to be developed? Do you have an interest in using digital storytelling as a way to create dialogue around topics you care about? Do you like making people laugh? Whether you are a regular Tik Tok creator or have never made a

video in your life, Digital Desmadre might be the place for you. We are looking for BIPOC performers, actors, and comedians between the ages of 17–25 to join our group and develop digital comedy sketches and digital shorts for social media platforms.[3]

The "Digital Desmadre" project consequently frames Borderlands Theater as providing a more intimate and collaborative community of creatives as well as a peer review process that supports emerging US Latinx playwrights and performers. The announcement explicitly states the project as part of Borderland Theater's mission to "create a space where a new generation of local BIPOC performers can grow their skills and build relationships with other young performers and Borderlands Theater" as well as "use art as a means of sparking civic dialogue around the pressing issues of our time."[4] Under the "commitment" description, applicants are told to expect once-a-week virtual meetings where they will "flesh out ideas, read scripts in development, and [participate in] general ensemble building" with the goal of "produc[ing] one digital short per month."[5] Notably, the theater makes a point of compensating for labor by paying performers a $50 stipend for their video appearances.

The videos posted on TikTok are part of a larger cohort shared on other social media sites, however, I will limit myself to these for the purposes of this essay. "We are not throwing away our shots!" is a parody of *Hamilton* and the original song where the main character establishes himself as the embodiment of American enterprise and upward mobility. In the parody, the performers sing about not throwing away their alcoholic beverages, clearly undercutting the original version's sober earnestness about national belonging. The second video, "MS 13," refers to the infamous international crime syndicate, "Mara Salvatrucha," and parodies the Fox News depiction of President Joe Biden as a terrorist threat. The video opens with a Latinx woman climbing onto a Stairmaster wearing a red hat and fanny pack with a cigarette in her mouth, performing the stereotype of a white MAGA supporter. As she furiously exercises, a browser window appears in the left-hand side of the screen, showing a clip of a Fox News anchor repeatedly warning that Biden's administration will "invite MS-13 to live next door."[6] Frightened, the screen turns black and white and the woman runs out into her suburban street to breathe a sigh of relief, until the camera returns to color and, for a split second, we see a headshot of a man dressed in a light blue bathrobe on whose face "Mara Salvatrucha" is written in black ink. Turns out MS-13 is already there, which calls into question the fear that the Biden administration will lead to the degradation of US society. The last post is also an original video, which responds to the pandemic's impact on US Latinx community, frontline workers, and employment power dynamics. In "Curbside Creep," a Latinx supermarket worker approaches a parked customer, with the sinister soundtrack from the shower scene in Hitchcock's film *Psycho* in the background. She asks, "can I get a name to confirm the order, please?" and then requests that he open the trunk of the car.[7] As the supermarket worker walks to the trunk, the driver gets out of the car and "creeps" over to silently watch her place the grocery bag inside. She looks at him, gets no response, and then turns to face the camera as she closes the trunk, whispering "what the fuck?" to the viewer. The video alludes to the physical dangers of frontline workers, often people of color, contrasting their experience with those who can afford to avoid that labor and exploit it for their own comfort and protection.

In addition to nurturing the creativity of a new generation of US Latinx playwrights and performers, Borderlands Theater prioritizes the archiving of US Latinx experiences. These projects are shared via the theater's primary social media venues, Instagram and Twitter, and their success is evidenced by the following numbers: 175 posts on Instagram with 1021 followers, and 1063 tweets on Twitter with 697 followers as of October 16, 2021. The series, "Stories: The Games We Played," collects the stories of US Latinx community elders sharing what they played as kids, in Spanish, English, and/or Spanglish. The description of the project mentions a couple of these games—"classic trompos, canicas, and bebeleche, to kick the can"—and prompts the viewer to consider "What did you do for fun as a kid?"[8] Emphasizing that "these games are taught at home and passed down generationally," Borderlands Theater encourages community members to "ask to be taught and take opportunities to teach" since these playful traditions "can only survive through us."[9]

The commitment to US Latinx community building, cultural expression, and archival practice is also evident in the oral history project, "Barrio Stories." The description explains that "Barrio Stories is a celebration of the history and heritage of Tucson's historic Mexican-American neighborhoods" that was "conceived by Borderlands Theater in 2015."[10] This "site-specific" archival project is "intended to preserve and reflect the stories, people, and places that made these barrios so vital to the cultural fabric of the Southwest" focusing on Barrio Viejo and Barrio Anita.[10] Videos include interviews with current and former residents who share "memories of growing up in the neighborhood" as well as audio files of talkbacks to live performances. These include video mapping, live music, and performance vignettes that reenact memories of the barrios, often staged in the lost spaces of the barrio. Assembling an archive also entails constructing the legacies of US Latinx playwrights, for example, the RAICES series of Borderlands Theater "features a circle of elders who share oral histories of art and culture of the Chicano movement in Tucson along with memories of Silviana Wood."[11]

The creative strategies of Borderlands Theater include collaborative projects with other institutions. During the pandemic, Borderlands Theater joined Teatros Unidos, "a national coalition of Latinx companies first assembled by Milagro Theatre" that enabled US Latinx theaters to survive economic challenges by "sharing resources and technical innovations to present virtual readings of new plays."[12] *Antigone at the Border* was one of these projects and as part of creating and staging the play, Borderlands Theater worked with Teatro Bravo, Su Teatro (Denver, CO), and Milagro (Portland, OR). Drawing from "interviews with DACA recipients and Latinx Border Patrol agents," the play depicted the impact of immigration policy on US Latinx communities in terms of both the "enforcers and enforced."[13] Additionally, a collaboration with StoryWorks led to the development of a documentary play by Milta Ortiz entitled *Cycles*, which was based on an investigation into "Arizona's foster care system."[14] A playwrights incubator program sponsored by Quetzal Guerrero and Borderlands Theater is currently supporting Milta Ortiz's development of *Anita*, "a musical in the universe of *Annie* with the Tucson sound."[15] While Borderlands Theater has only shared three videos via TikTok thus far, their clearly articulated artistic mission and astounding diversity of their community endeavors means that the organization is poised to make a great impact on this additional platform.

Thriving: Gabriel Rodriguez and @genuinelygabriel

As I mentioned at the opening of this chapter, TikTok accounts of US Latinx individuals offer another perspective on how the platform functions as an intervention into the theater world(s). Those who identify as US Latinx theater performers often offer important, insightful critiques about the casting of BIPOC performers in mainstream theater by US Latinx actors, for example, @gabriela_chiriboga's post "White Latinx actors using 'POC status' to get cast" and @pr_baby_jesus's post "A former racist direvtor [sic]." Many accounts speak to the experiences of BIPOC people in a white dominant theater tradition, for example, @reachingalw discusses the musicals of Andrew

Lloyd Weber or @giz_zy promoting a production of *Frozen*. At the same time, US Latinx content creators on TikTok rarely reference US Latinx playwrights. It is disheartening to see a generation of Latinx creatives who remain unaware of the vibrant US Latinx theatrical traditions and the contemporary institutions that keep them alive and growing. Systemic racism in education and theater is one of the many obstacles to the acquisition of knowledge about the histories of US Latinx theater as well as participation in the production of US Latinx plays. The disconnect makes clear why the work of an educator like @genuinelygabriel is so necessary.

As the originator of hashtags such as #DiversePlays and #LatinxPlays, Gabriel Rodriguez[16] is a trailblazer who is building an archive of videos via @genuinelygabriel about important BIPOC playwrights whose "diverse shows you didn't learn about in your theater program!" Rodriguez's TikTok account is part of a broader effort by an organization he co-founded, The Diverse Theater Initiative. A cursory review of the initiative's various projects appears to indicate that he is the current director and I therefore read the TikTok posts by @genuinelygabriel as single-authored by Rodriguez. His account's reach is much more expansive than that of the theaters I've discussed in this chapter, with 1,432 followers and 16.9K likes as of October 16, 2021. The #DiversePlays series includes over 60 posts and those that are labeled with #LatinxPlays number about 17. The videos highlight one work by a US Latinx playwright, providing a general plot summary of the play and an overview of the major themes it addresses. These posts seek to raise awareness about the variety of perspectives and topics covered by US Latinx theater and encourage viewers to seek out the work of these playwrights to learn more. The @genuinelygabriel account is a curated canon that includes Josefina López's *Real Women Have Curves*, Nilo Cruz's *Anna in the Tropics*, José Cruz González's *American Mariachi*, Karen Zacarías's *Just Like Us* and *Native Gardens*, Kristoffer Díaz's *The Elaborate Entrance of Chad Deity*, John Leguizamo's *Latin History for Morons*, José Rivera's *Marisol*, Tanya Saracho's *Fade*, Christina Quintana's *Enter Into Your Sleep*, Luis Alfaro's *Electricidad*, Quiara Alegría Hudes's *Water by the Spoonful*, and María Irene Fornés's *Letters from Cuba*, *Conduct of Life*, and *Dr. Keal*. Rodriguez emphasizes that these well-established playwrights are not part of the American theater tradition taught at universities. While the activist project of @genuinelygabriel makes an important intervention, his counternarrative is dominated by the most recent generation of writers, especially those who are producing their work in US Latinx theaters across the country. A major limitation to the circulation of US Latinx plays is that few playwrights are able to have their scripts published. Access matters: it is the publication and press marketing of individual plays and anthologies that facilitate the path from the stage to the classroom. Playwrights whose work is in print are more likely to be read and taught by faculty.

Conclusion

And so, dear reader, what are we going to do about the disconnect on TikTok and elsewhere on social media between these different communities invested in US Latinx theater, between performers, teachers, and theaters? We need to amplify the work of US Latinx theaters, the institutions dedicated to community building and the production of US Latinx shows like Teatro Audaz of San Antonio, Teatro Bravo in Phoenix, Borderlands Theater of Tucson, Teatro 8 of Miami, and Quemoción Production Company. We need to populate hashtags like #DiversePlays, #LatinxPlays, #LatinxPlaywright, #LatinxActor, #LatinxDirector, and #LatinxTheater with original content that showcases US Latinx playwrights and the organizations that genuinely make space for their work and foster creativity. We need to generate new hashtags and content dedicated to AfroLatinx, Chicano, Nuyorican, and Puerto Rican theater and playwrights, as well as US Latinx creatives of other ethnicities. We need to spread the word about the individuals and organizations already doing this kind of generous, heart-felt, and difficult labor. Clearly, we have quite a bit of work to do. Let's get started!

Notes

1 Quemoción Production Company (@quemocion), "Los Muros: A Conversation with Henry Dominguez," TikTok, posted February 19, accessed October 16, 2021, https://www.tiktok.com/@quemocion/video/6931203338486729989.
2 Quemoción Production Company (@quemocion), "'Soldaderas' by Yasmin Hernández (Part 1)," TikTok, posted July 22, accessed October 16, 2021, https://www.tiktok.com/@quemocion/video/6987834282408430854.
3 Borderlands Theater, "Digital Desmadre," Borderlands Theater, last modified April 15, 2021, accessed October 16, 2021, http://www.borderlandstheater.org/digital-demadre/.
4 Ibid.
5 Ibid.
6 Borderlands Theater (@digitaldesmadre), "MS 13," TikTok, October 17, 2020, https://www.tiktok.com/@digitaldesmadre/video/6884611765892549893.

7 Borderlands Theater (@digitaldesmadre), "Creep," TikTok, posted March 2, accessed October 16, 2021, https://www.tiktok.com/@digitaldesmadre/video/6935055122783407366.

8 Borderlands Theater, "Barrio Stories: The Games We Played," Facebook, posted June 25, accessed October 16, 2021, https://mtouch.facebook.com/story.php?story_fbid=4222619617780801&id=212306712145465&m_entstream_source=timeline.

9 Borderlands Theater, "Barrio Stories: The Games We Played," Facebook, posted June 25, accessed October 16, 2021, https://mtouch.facebook.com/story.php?story_fbid=4222619617780801&id=212306712145465&m_entstream_source=timeline.

10 Borderlands Theater, "Barrio Stories," Borderlands Theater, accessed October 16, 2021, http://www.barriostories.org/.

11 Borderlands Theater, "Amor de Hija/Tribute to Silviana Wood," Borderlands Theater, August 15, 2020, http://www.borderlandstheater.org/amor-de-hija-tribute-to-silviana-wood/.

12 Borderlands Theater, "Collaborating Through the Covid Crisis," Borderlands Theater, August 19, 2020, http://www.borderlandstheater.org/collaborating-through-covid/.

13 Borderlands Theater, "Antigone at the Border," Borderlands Theater, January 24, 2021, http://www.borderlandstheater.org/antigone-at-the-border/.

14 Borderlands Theater, "Cycles," Borderlands Theater, January 14, 2021, http://www.borderlandstheater.org/cycles/.

15 Milta Ortiz, "About Me," accessed October 16, 2021, https://miltaortiz.com/about.

16 The Diverse Theater Initiative, "On the Road to Joy & Freedom," The Diverse Theatre Initiative, accessed on October 16, 2021, https://www.thedti.org/on-the-road-to-joy-and-freedom.

Afterword

TikTok Industrial Complex; or Twenty-First-Century Transculturative Creative Critical Collaboratory?

Frederick Luis Aldama

When you're working at the avantgarde of pop culture, so much changes minute by minute. It's hard to know where or even how to insert one's critical, scholarly eye in ways that will generate knowledge. Indeed, as Trevor Boffone's elegant and learned introduction reminds us, it's easy to miss the emergence of culture in its process of in-the-moment shaping, happening, and innovating. Insert we do—and must—in the absolute present moment of the global pop cultural phenomenon that is, TikTok. As the remarkable scholars of TikTok herein attest, we can create concepts to make sense and generate knowledge anew that enriches understanding of TikTok as a technology of culture making and engaging—*poieses*, per the Ancient Greeks—that speaks deeply to our existence as *homo faber*.

TikTok has been studied. However, the questions, methods, and approaches have largely grown out of the social, behavioral, and health sciences—fields generally that have shaped it into a branch of critical technocultural discourse studies focused on algorithms, influence, and mental health. Boffone and this extraordinary league of TikTok scholars approach the subject from a humanistic angle, asking questions that gravitate around issues of who we are as humans and our humanity, including explorations of how we give shape to cultural phenomena in and through TikTok; how TikTok shapes the world; and how this newly shaped world transforms us. More specifically, Boffone and this coterie of scholars put front and center inquiries and explorations oft swept to the margins of scholarly inquiry such as how the making and engaging of TikTok cultures spin out of ethnoracial, gender, and queer subjectivities to shape epistemologies anew.

TikTok is a technology that allows anyone with a TikTok account to spin out of themselves and give shape to information, story, music, performance, art—all cultural phenomena. But let me take pause here

DOI: 10.4324/9781003280705-15

to reflect briefly on what culture is. For this I turn to Cuban polymath, Fernando Ortiz's dual concepts of social syncretism and transculturation. In *Cuban Counterpoint: Tobacco and Sugar* (1995), Cuba's sugar and tobacco industries led him to ask questions of culture and culture making. With eyes wide open to the exploitation and genocide created by these profit-making industries, he wanted to understand better how the contact (forced or otherwise) of Black, mestizo, indigenous, and EuroSpanish peninsulars created a convergence then emergence of a new, third culture: Cubanidad or Cubanness.

Ortega's approach and concept continues to be remarkably generative, especially as focused on the new, third transcultures created by TikTokers. TikTok is transculturation apotheosized, with the direct and indirect (digital) contact of human beings and human groups at once in permanence and perpetual transformation, always changing in spatial and temporal motion. TikTok is conservative and in flux, always transcending and morphing into something new. TikTok is a shaping technology where planetary peoples and cultures reverberatively intersect, exchange, and then create something new.

As the scholarship herein shows, the careful study of TikTok allows us to understand better its addictive and transformative presence in our lives. The scholarship opens ways that we can breakdown its form and content elements into constituent parts and then rebuild them into a whole to understand better society in and through its: consumption, reception, and production practices; technologies of identity shaping, exploration, and performing; making of knowledge repositories by those subjects otherwise discarded, shunned, unseen, and unheard.

My pinned TikToks include #Latino, #Latina, #Familia and #Comida, #CulturaPop, #Familia, #ComicBook, #Education, #LGBTQ, #Undocu, and #BookTok, among others. With Fernandes Cortes (@fernandacortesx), one can learn not only of canonical pre-Columbian and post-conquest Mexican mythical figures, healers, and heroes like La Catrina and Chavela Vargas but also of arguably lesser known "Bad A** Latinas in History" like La Moneja de Durango, Afrolatina La Mulata de Córdoba, and Sylvia Rivera—the Rosa Parks of the Modern Transgender Movement. With #Undocumented, one can find information, performance art, storytelling, and calls to collective action that crisscross race, ethnic, gender, and sexuality identities.

While I'm mostly in awe at how such an extreme time constraint—15 or 60 seconds and now three minutes—can and does make for some incredible results. I use TikTok in my classroom, and to great, joyous results. I use it as a tool to disseminate knowledge about all things of Latinx pop culture. I assign it to my students to review concepts and shape knowledge. Halfway through my undergraduate courses, I devote a class period to a TikTok Maker Studio session, assigning to groups of two the task of creating a one-minute TikTok focused on a concept, category, or narrative tool learned for class. With lots of laughter and smiles, students review, master, and then redeploy their knowledge about film, TV, comic books—Latinx pop culture generally.

This said, just like all cultural phenomenon, not all TikToks are made the same. As I discuss elsewhere in my work, TikTok cultural phenomenon is made with greater or lesser degrees of a will to style. By this I mean, how a given TikTok content creator brings a high (or low) degree of skill in the application of the different devices available in the shaping of their respective TikTok object. And the TikTok content creator brings different degrees of a sense of *responsibility* to the distillation and reconstruction of the building blocks of reality they choose to focus on. Put simply, some TikTok cultural objects are careless, lazy, unoriginal (egregiously appropriative), narcissistic, and deliberate gaslight peddlers of misinformation. A case in point, all those white TikTokers who appropriated then were rewarded for stealing Black TikTok dance performances (#BlackTikTokStrike).

I haven't completely chugged the TikTok Kool-Aid. Like the scholars in this volume, I see with eyes wide open TikTok's dark side. There's the cringe-video phenomenon used to bully and mark individuals and groups; there's the data gathering that leads to racial profiling and digital redlining; there's the hypersexualization of women and demonizing of Blacks, Latinx, Asian, Indigenous, and LGBTQ peoples. And, not all people across the globe have access to TikTok, reminding us that we live in a world where fewer and fewer have access to technologies, literacies, and resources to realize their full potentialities as shapers and active engagers of culture.

TikTok is *not* a nonprofit out to transform for the better our planet. It is a corporate behemoth (ByteDance) that uses nefarious algorithms and exploitative structures (sponsorships) and promises (TikTok mansions) in ways that perpetuate systems of oppression, racism, classism, sexism as well as trans and queerphobia.

Recently, a vandalism challenge posted on TikTok (#DeviantLicks) blazed across high schools in the United States. It led to all sorts of mischief making. However, the real TikTok challenge for us *all* is to see how we can use it as *tool* for creating collaboratories for transculturative art and knowledge production. The challenge is to bring a transcultural analytic approach to TikTok that points to the crucial moments of change and cultural transformation that gives rise to something new through a specific process of cultural creation and innovation. The challenge is to see TikTok as a transcultural phenomenon and as a series of convergences, movements, and innovative emergences that unfold across the globe in syncopated, synergistic rhythms of cultural contact and encounter.

The real TikTok challenge, then, is to assert the importance of sociohistorical facts and realities all while understanding that its transculturative products are transient and provisional—always unadjusted and readjusting. Whether Gen Z or Gen-Whatever, what this volume's scholars model so elegantly is the possible pathways that we can pursue to realize these challenges and understand TikTok as a twenty-first-century transculturative and transformative creative critical collaboratory.

Index

132 *Index*

For Product Safety Concerns and Information please contact our EU
representative GPSR@taylorandfrancis.com
Taylor & Francis Verlag GmbH, Kaufingerstraße 24, 80331 München, Germany

www.ingramcontent.com/pod-product-compliance
Lightning Source LLC
Chambersburg PA
CBHW061747270326
41928CB00011B/2404